Know Chocolate for Lent
A Resource for Congregations

Anna L. Liechty & Phyllis Vos Wezeman

LeaderResources Leeds, MA

Dedication

To Mary Gifford ...

... fellow chocoholic, for all the Lenten seasons we were deprived of chocolate's inspiration! A.L.L.

To Linda Babcock ...

... A lover of chocolate! A lover of life! P.V.W.

Thanks

Ronald W. Liechty and Kenneth R. Wezeman ...

... for technical and theological support

Margaret M. Eggleston ...

... for design and illustration

Know Chocolate for Lent
A Resource for Congregations
Anna L. Liechty and Phyllis Vos Wezeman

Copyright 2009
Active Learning Associates, Inc.
ISBN 978-1-59518-037-7

Publisher
LeaderResources
P. O. Box 302
Leeds, MA 01053
1-800-941-2218
Staff@LeaderResources.Org
www.LeaderResources.Org

Table of Contents

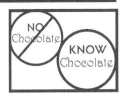

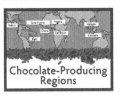

Chocolate-Producing Regions

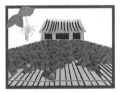

Table of Contents

Introduction

Know Chocolate for Lent: A Resource for Congregations offers a thematic approach for communicating the message of the Church Seasons of Lent and Easter. *Know Chocolate for Lent* uses the growing and manufacturing process of chocolate as a metaphor for the growth of faith and discipleship in the Christian life. Lent is an appropriate time for reflection and study so that believers comprehend the significance of the life, death, and resurrection of Jesus Christ. *Know Chocolate for Lent* helps congregations reflect on the significance of the gifts that they often take for granted—the gift of chocolate and the gift of faith.

Through their participation, people of all ages will experience the connections between the growing process of chocolate and the growing process of being a Christian. They will connect God's gift of the rainforest and God's gift of the Church. In addition, they will understand that what they often take for granted—whether it is chocolate or faith—is much more satisfying when they know the story behind the traditions they celebrate.

An overview of the components of *Know Chocolate for Lent: A Resource for Congregations* for the six weeks of Lent as well as the special days of Ash Wednesday, Maundy Thursday, Good Friday, and Easter Sunday is provided.

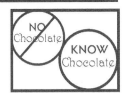

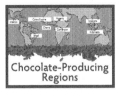

Chocolate-Producing Regions

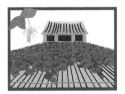

Week	Word	Theme	Scripture	Chart	Chocolate
Ash Wednesday	Know What	Know What we often take for granted	Matthew 6:1-6, 16-21 2 Corinthians 5:20b-6:10	NO Chocolate/ KNOW Chocolate	Chocolate
First Sunday in Lent	Know Where	Know Where the best growth occurs	Mark 1:9-15 I Peter 3:18-22	World map of chocolate-producing regions	Chocolate kisses Wrappers from chocolate products
Second Sunday in Lent	Know How	Know How being different is a blessing	Mark 8:31-38 Romans 4:13-25	Cacao tree with blossoms and pods	M&M'S®
Third Sunday in Lent	Know Which	Know Which part of life is most important	John 2:13-22 1 Corinthians 1:18-25	Open cacao pod revealing seeds	Chocolate covered cacao or coffee beans
Fourth Sunday in Lent	Know When	Know When it's time to share good news	John 3:14-21 Ephesians 2:1-10	Cacao beans ready for fermenting	Hot chocolate mix
Fifth Sunday in Lent	Know Why	Know Why health benefits both body and soul	Luke 17:6-7 Hebrews 11:1-3	Dried cacao beans	Dark chocolate bars
Sixth Sunday in Lent (Palm/Passion)	Know So	Know So choices can be based on wisdom	Matthew 21:1-11 Philippians 2:5-11	Crushed cacao beans	Chocolate mini-bars
Maundy Thursday	Know By	Know By remembering Jesus' words and deeds	John 13:21-30 1 Corinthians 11:23-26	Advertisement for heart-shaped box of chocolates	Heart-shaped box of chocolates
Good Friday	Know That	Know That something bitter can make things better	John 19:16-18 Hebrews 19:19-23	Symbol for fair trade chocolate	Fair trade chocolate
Easter Sunday	Know Who	Know Who calls to us in faith	John 20:1-18 1 Corinthians 15:1-11	Final product	White chocolate bunny, cross, egg, or lamb

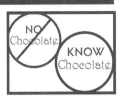

Overview

Components

   Altar or Worship Center Arrangement

   Banner or Posters

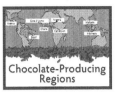

   Children's Messages

   Scripture

   Sermons

   Teaching Tools

Supplies

Advance Preparation

   Banner or Posters

   Worship Center Arrangement

Leadership

Enhancements

Children's Messages

   Ash Wednesday: Know What

   First Sunday in Lent: Know Where

   Second Sunday in Lent: Know How

   Third Sunday in Lent: Know Which

   Fourth Sunday in Lent: Know When

   Fifth Sunday in Lent: Know Why

   Sixth Sunday in Lent (Palm Sunday/Passion Sunday): Know So

   Maundy Thursday: Know By

   Good Friday: Know That

   Easter Sunday: Know Who

Know Chocolate for Lent: A Resource for Congregations provides the focus for a wide variety of seasonal experiences including: creating visuals, decorating worship centers, providing special holiday services, preaching sermons, reading Scripture, sharing children's messages, and making visual and concrete the goodness of God's gifts. In addition to weekly worship helps, the book includes family devotions and activities for the six Sundays and the special days of Lent and Easter.

In order to use the thematic approach offered in *Know Chocolate for Lent*, the committee or people coordinating the Lent and Easter programming and decorating must adapt the elements provided to best fit the individual congregation's needs. Any or all of the following components may be used to enhance the preparation for and the celebration of the resurrection of Christ.

Components

Altar or Worship Center Arrangement

A visual display could be created as a focal point for worship during Lent and Easter. One possibility would be to design a rainforest environment as a background for the altar or worship center arrangement. Each week the symbol suggested in the Chart portion of the children's message—and provided as an illustration/pattern in the Enhancements section of this resource—could be added to the display. As an alternative or an addition to the graphics, actual photos or scientific models of the symbols could be used. Consideration must be given to the dimensions of the sanctuary when determining size and placement of the display.

Banner or Posters

Illustrations for the symbols suggested in the Chart portion of the children's messages are included in the Enhancements section of this resource. Use these graphics to create a banner or a set of posters for the special days and Sundays of the seasons of Lent and Easter. Each visual helps to reinforce the theme for the day and serves as a reminder of the lesson. They include:

Ash Wednesday: Know What

   NO Chocolate/KNOW Chocolate

First Sunday in Lent: Know Where

   World map depicting chocolate-producing regions

Second Sunday in Lent: Know How

   Cacao tree with blossoms and pods

Third Sunday in Lent: Know Which

   Open cacao pod revealing seeds

Fourth Sunday in Lent: Know When

   Cacao beans ready for fermenting

Fifth Sunday in Lent: Know Why

   Dried cacao beans

Sixth Sunday in Lent (Palm Sunday/Passion Sunday): Know So

   Crushed cacao beans

Maundy Thursday: Know By

    Advertisement for heart-shaped box of chocolates

Good Friday: Know That

    Symbol for fair trade chocolate

Easter Sunday: Know Who

    Final product—white chocolate bunny, cross, egg, or lamb

Children's Messages

Ten children's messages are included, one each for the six Sundays of Lent, plus the four special days of Ash Wednesday, Maundy Thursday, Good Friday, and Easter. The messages may be given as a part of the morning worship service, used as a segment of Children's Church, or offered as devotions for Sunday School classes or mid-week programs. If the Ash Wednesday message is not used on that day, be sure to incorporate the introduction to the theme and the explanation for the season into the previous Sunday's children's sermon or into the children's message for the First Sunday in Lent.

Each children's message outline contains several sections. They include:

Challenge
    Conveys the theme of the story as it relates to the week's Lent or Easter message.

Chapter
    Lists the Scripture readings that focus on the theme.

Chart
    Provides the symbol connected with the theme.

Chocolate
    Suggests the chocolate items to offer to participants.

Chat
    Offers a suggested script for the children's sermon and a prayer to conclude the children's time.

Scripture

Scripture lessons for the Sundays and special days of Lent and Easter are taken from the Gospels and the Epistles. All themes correlate with, but are not based on, the Revised Common Lectionary passages for Years A, B, and C. They include:

Ash Wednesday: Know What
    Matthew 6:1-6, 16-21
    2 Corinthians 5:20b-6:10

First Sunday in Lent: Know Where
    Mark 1:9-15
    1 Peter 3:18-22

Second Sunday in Lent: Know How
    Mark 8:31-38
    Romans 4:13-25

Third Sunday in Lent: Know Which
    John 2:13-22
    1 Corinthians 1:18-25

Fourth Sunday in Lent: Know When
  John 3:14-21
  Ephesians 2:1-10

Fifth Sunday in Lent: Know Why
  Luke 17:6-7
  Hebrews 11:1-3

Sixth Sunday in Lent (Palm Sunday/Passion Sunday): Know So
  Matthew 21:1-11
  Philippians 2:5-11

Maundy Thursday: Know By
  John 13:21-30
  1 Corinthians 11:23-26

Good Friday: Know That
  John 19:16-18
  Hebrews 10:19-23

Easter Sunday: Know Who
  John 20:1-18
  1 Corinthians 15:1-11

Sermons

Each theme may be used as a springboard for developing a sermon appropriate to the week's emphasis. They include:

Ash Wednesday: Know What

  Know What we often take for granted
  Our Lenten commitment to "know chocolate" challenges us to recognize that we often take life's best gifts for granted—whether it is chocolate or God's loving presence.

First Sunday in Lent: Know Where

  Know Where the best growth occurs
  Our Lenten commitment to "know chocolate" challenges us to acknowledge God's plan for providing growing conditions—both in the rainforest and in the Church.

Second Sunday in Lent: Know How

  Know How being different is a blessing
  Our Lenten commitment to "know chocolate" challenges us to embrace the differences that make God's creation unique—both for the cacao tree and for the Christian disciple.

Third Sunday in Lent: Know Which

  Know Which part of life is most important
  Our Lenten commitment to "know chocolate" challenges us to envision the potential for changing the world—both with chocolate and with God's love.

Fourth Sunday in Lent: Know When

  Know When it's time to share good news
  Our Lenten commitment to "know chocolate" challenges us to share goodness with the world—both the recipes for chocolate delicacies and God's good news of Jesus Christ.

Fifth Sunday in Lent: Know Why

Know Why health benefits both body and soul
Our Lenten commitment to "know chocolate" challenges us to understand that God wants us to be healthy—both physically and spiritually.

Sixth Sunday in Lent (Palm Sunday/Passion Sunday): Know So

Know So choices can be based on wisdom
Our Lenten commitment to "know chocolate" challenges us to distinguish the genuine from the imitation—both in types of chocolates and in those we choose to follow.

Maundy Thursday: Know By

Know By remembering Jesus' words and deeds
Our Lenten commitment to "know chocolate" challenges us to remember those we love on special occasions—both with gifts of chocolate and with gifts of bread and cup.

Good Friday: Know That

Know That something bitter can make things better
Our Lenten commitment to "know chocolate" challenges us to accept that God can use what is bitter to produce something good—both in the taste of chocolate and in the life of Jesus.

Easter Sunday: Know Who

Know Who calls us to follow in faith
Our Lenten commitment to "know chocolate" challenges us to learn the difference that can happen when we are open to change—just like the process that can make white chocolate or the miracle of resurrection that can make new life.

Teaching Tools

In addition to the weekly Chart, or illustration, associated with the theme for Ash Wednesday, the six weeks of Lent, Maundy Thursday, Good Friday, and Easter Sunday, an additional teaching tool may be part of the presentation for the children's message. In addition, a chocolate item is offered to the participants after the closing prayer. They include:

Ash Wednesday: Know What
    Chocolate kisses
    Wrappers from chocolate products

First Sunday in Lent: Know Where
    Milk chocolate bars

Second Sunday in Lent: Know How
    M&M'S®

Third Sunday in Lent: Know Which
    Chocolate covered cacao or coffee beans

Fourth Sunday in Lent: Know When
    Hot chocolate mix

Fifth Sunday in Lent: Know Why
    Dark chocolate bars

Sixth Sunday in Lent (Palm Sunday/Passion Sunday): Know So
    Chocolate mini-bars

Maundy Thursday: Know By
   Heart-shaped box of chocolates

Good Friday: Know That
   Fair trade chocolate

Easter Sunday: Know Who
   White chocolate bunny, cross, egg, or lamb

Supplies

To create the visual display, to prepare the components of *Know Chocolate for Lent*, and to share the children's messages, the coordinator must assemble the following materials:

banner or posters,
Bible,
items for worship center arrangement,
teaching tools for children's messages.

Advance Preparation

Banner or Posters

Construct a banner or individual posters for each symbol suggested in the Chart portion of the children's sermon. Refer to the Enhancements section of this resource for banner making instructions and for reproducible illustrations.

Worship Center Arrangement

Choose an area to serve as the focal point for a seasonal worship center arrangement. Cover an altar, display area, or table with purple cloth for the season of Lent and with white fabric for Easter Sunday.

As a basic display, suggest a rainforest environment with green plants of varying heights to suggest the layers of vegetation.

Additional ideas for the worship center arrangement might include:

depicting the stages of the chocolate process with drawings or photographs.
displaying the theme words for each week.
setting objects representing the symbols in the worship center arrangement.

Leadership

Coordination of *Know Chocolate for Lent* can be done by one person, or duties may be assigned to staff such as Pastors or Christian Education Directors as well as volunteers serving on Seasonal Task Forces or Worship Committees.

Whoever assumes responsibility must see that leadership is provided for:

coordinating decorations,
creating visual displays,
facilitating special events,
leading special worship services,
reading Scripture,
sharing children's messages.

Enhancements

Know Chocolate for Lent may be used as a worship theme for Lent and Easter, or may be used extensively to provide the framework for coordinating congregational life during these seasons. The theme may be enhanced beyond worship applications to include education, nurture, and outreach opportunities.

Children's Messages
Ash Wednesday: Know What

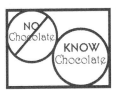

Challenge

Know What
Know What we often take for granted
Our Lenten commitment to "know chocolate" challenges us to recognize that we often take life's best gifts for granted—whether it is chocolate or God's loving presence.

Chapter

Matthew 6:1-6, 16-21
2 Corinthians 5:20b-6:10

Chart

NO Chocolate/KNOW Chocolate

Chocolate

Chocolate kisses
Wrappers from chocolate products

Chat

Do you recognize any of these wrappers?

[Hold up empty chocolate wrappers.]

Too bad these are empty! Is one of these a favorite of yours?

[Allow suggestions of favorites.]

Have you ever heard anyone say that he or she plans to give up chocolate for Lent? Yes? No? Since today is Ash Wednesday, the first day of the forty-day season called Lent, you just might hear folks say that there will be NO chocolate until Easter arrives. Giving up something we find tempting—especially chocolate—is one way to discipline our spirits as we prepare for Easter. We make a sacrifice in order to better understand the sacrifice Jesus made for us. But during this Lenten season, I want to suggest a different way to prepare for Easter. Instead of NO – N-O—chocolate for Lent, how about KNOW – K–N–O–W—chocolate for Lent?

[Display both sides of the chart as the words NO Chocolate and KNOW Chocolate are spoken and spelled.]

We can get ready for Easter by learning about God's gift of chocolate as we prepare to receive God's gift of Jesus' life, death, and resurrection. So this year we want to know chocolate for Lent. Say it with me: Know chocolate for Lent.

[Hold up KNOW Chocolate side of chart.]

If you agree to our challenge to know chocolate for Lent, then I have a question for you on this Ash Wednesday. When you enjoy chocolate do you ever think about where the candy comes from? How and where does chocolate grow? Who works hard so that we can have a chocolate bar whenever we want? Most of us eat our favorite candy without thinking about who makes chocolate possible. Without the season of Lent, we might treat Easter the same way. We might just enjoy the good news of Jesus' resurrection and never stop to understand or appreciate how that amazing story of the empty tomb came to be or what Jesus' sacrifice means to each of us.

This year during Lent, let's take the time to learn to know chocolate and to know the story of Jesus. On Ash Wednesday, these empty wrappers can remind us that today we begin our journey toward an empty tomb. As we begin our journey we can seal our promise to know chocolate with a kiss.

[Hold up a foil-wrapped chocolate kiss.]

But first, let's talk to God together.

Dear God, Help us to know that all good things come from You. During Lent, may we empty our lives to be filled by Your goodness. Amen.

[As the children are dismissed, offer one or two foil-wrapped chocolate kisses to each participant.]

Children's Messages
First Sunday in Lent: Know Where

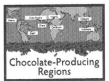

Chocolate-Producing Regions

Challenge

Know Where
Know Where the best growth occurs
Our Lenten commitment to "know chocolate" challenges us to acknowledge God's plan for providing growing conditions—both in the rainforest and in the Church.

Chapter

Mark 1:9-15
1 Peter 3:18-22

Chart

World map depicting chocolate-producing regions

Chocolate

Milk chocolate bars

Chat

Aren't you glad that during Lent we agreed that, instead of NO [N-O] chocolate, we would KNOW [K-N-O-W] chocolate?!? Let's begin by discovering where chocolate grows. Are chocolate bars picked from bushes that grow just anywhere? No … that's silly, isn't it! But chocolate does begin by growing on a tree, on the cacao [kah-COW] plant to be exact. And the cacao plant can only grow in a special part of the world. Does anyone know where on this map the cacao tree grows?

[Hold up the world map depicting chocolate-producing regions and let a volunteer point to several countries.]

There must be very special growing conditions for chocolate. The cacao tree can only develop within twenty degrees of the equator.

[Point out the appropriate latitudes around the equator.]

So that means the plant grows only around the middle area of the earth—like a belt—in a place called the rainforest.

The rainforest is an ecosystem. Does anyone know what that means?

[Guide responses so that all understand the interactive relationship of plants, animals, insects, and environment that create an ecosystem.]

So the cacao plant can only grow in a place that is warm and moist, in a place where a canopy of leaves provides the tender plant some shade and protection, in a place with tiny insects that can pollinate the cacao plant's flowers. The rainforest is the perfect place for the cacao plant to receive everything it needs in order to grow, bloom, and produce the seed pods that people harvest to make chocolate. Everything in the ecosystem works together for good, just as our Creator God planned.

So, where does chocolate grow? In the rainforest! Say it with me: In the rainforest!

During Lent, as we come to know chocolate, we also come to know more about our Lenten journey of faith. If chocolate grows in the rainforest, where do Christians grow?

[Hint: Where are we on this First Sunday of Lent? The Church.]

Yes! The Church! If we think about it, the Church is like a rainforest. The water of baptism and the warmth of the Holy Spirit unite God's people. Each of us plays a different but important role in the ecosystem called the Church. The Church doesn't only exist near the equator though. God's Church is scattered all over the world. However, in order to survive the Church must remain close to God. God is like the equator—the source that runs through the middle of everything we are and everything we do. So now you know the first Lenten lesson: Where does chocolate grow? Say it with me: The rainforest! Where do Christians grow? Say it with me: The Church! I think that deserves a know chocolate reward!

[Hold up a small milk chocolate bar.]

But first, let's talk to God together.

Dear God, Thank You for creating all the right conditions for us to grow in faith. Help us to value the role each one plays in Your Church. Amen.

[As the children are dismissed, distribute a small milk chocolate bar or section to each participant.]

Children's Messages
Second Sunday in Lent: Know How

Challenge

Know How
Know How being different is a blessing
Our Lenten commitment to "know chocolate" challenges us to embrace the differences that make God's creation unique—both for the cacao tree and for the Christian disciple.

Chapter

Mark 8:31-38
Romans 4:13-25

Chart

Cacao tree with blossoms and pods

Chocolate

M&M'S®

Chat

From our last chat, we now know that chocolate grows in the—rainforest! Right! And Christians grow in the—Church! Yes! But how does chocolate grow? That's what we need to know on this Second Sunday in Lent as we journey together toward Easter. If I gave you a piece of paper and asked you to draw a picture of a cacao tree, what would you draw? Close your eyes and imagine what a chocolate plant might look like. Can you see the tree in your mind's eye?

[Hold up a picture or a model of a cacao tree with blossoms and pods.]

Open your eyes! Did your imagined tree look like this?

[Ask the participants to describe one thing they notice about the cacao tree that they might not have imagined.]

Some people find the real cacao tree a rather surprising creation. It is certainly different than most other trees we know.

[If possible, point to examples on the picture or model of each item described.]

First of all, the cacao tree blossoms all year long, not just at certain times or seasons. And the blossoms can occur any place on the tree—usually the flowers are directly attached to the trunk. Flying all around the blooms are the tiny midge flies that pollinate the blossoms so that they can grow into football-shaped pods the size of pineapples. Those pods are what people harvest so that we can have chocolate! The cacao tree is certainly different from the other trees of the world, isn't it? It blooms everywhere and all the time! Say it with me: Everywhere! All the time!

The more we know the story of chocolate, the more connections we have to think about during Lent. Do you know how Christians grow? In many ways, Christians are to bloom just like the cacao tree. We are to blossom all year round. That means others should see the beauty of God's presence in our lives—not just for a little while or just on Sunday mornings, but all the time. And we blossom best when we are attached directly to God, just like those flowers on the trunk of this tree. And while all those flies might seem like problems, they are important to help the tree produce fruit. Likewise, the problems that beset us in life are the ones that help us produce the fruit of faith. Jesus didn't promise His followers an easy life. He challenges us to pick up our cross and follow in faith. If we do that, then our lives, too, will produce fruit that benefits the world around us. We may be different than the rest of the world who doesn't know God, but that's okay! In Lent, we celebrate that being a Christian makes us different, but we learn to let our lives bloom with God's love right where we are. So where do Christians bloom? Everywhere! And when? All the time! Sounds like you know chocolate—and the life of faith. Let's celebrate with a chocolate connection that we can share easily everywhere and all the time!

[Hold up a package of M&M'S®.]

But first, let's talk to God together.

Dear God, Thank You for Your love that flows through us all the time. Help us to blossom with faith everywhere we go. Amen.

[As the children are dismissed, distribute a small bag of M&M'S® to each participant.]

Children's Messages
Third Sunday in Lent: Know Which

Challenge

Know Which
Know Which part of life is most important
Our Lenten commitment to "know chocolate" challenges us to envision the potential for changing the world – both with chocolate and with God's love.

Chapter

John 2:13-22
1 Corinthians 1:18-25

Chart

Open cacao pod revealing seeds

Chocolate

Chocolate covered cacao or coffee beans

Chat

From our last chat, we know that chocolate and Christians produce fruit in the same way: Everywhere! All the time! But what do we know about the fruit of the cacao tree? Which do the pods produce—beans or seeds?

[Hold up a picture or a model of an open cacao pod revealing seeds.]

Although some people might call what is inside each pod a bean, we will call them seeds because they can be planted to produce more cacao trees. Each football-shaped cacao pod contains about thirty to fifty almond-sized seeds. That's enough to make seven milk chocolate candy bars! About 2,000 years ago, the ancient people known as the Maya began gathering cacao seeds from rainforest trees and planting this important crop in their gardens. Cacao seeds were so important they were even used as money for shopping at the market. Later the Aztecs learned about the wonders of cacao seeds from the Mayan people. Still later, the Spanish carried many treasures back to Europe—including cacao seeds and the recipe for the Aztec chocolate drink. The seeds, which are inside the cacao pod, are the most important part because we make chocolate from them. But even more importantly, we can also plant the seeds to grow more cacao trees!

If every pod on every cacao tree produces thirty to fifty seeds, and each of those seeds produces a tree that produces hundreds of pods that each contain thirty to fifty seeds … Oh my! I don't think I can count that high! So when we look at one cacao seed, we can see one seed or we can see a tree that produces more pods than we can count, each with more seeds than we can count! Imagine the first Mayan family that tended a cacao tree in their garden. They simply could not have dreamed how that one act would influence their nation, the nation of the Aztecs, and then the Spanish, and then all of Europe, and then America, and then you and me! All because someone realized that what's on the inside matters most. So what do we know about the cacao seed?

[Refer to the picture or model of the open cacao pod with seeds.]

Say it with me: What's on the inside matters most.

During Lent, that is also what we need to know about being a Christian. Each of us is like a seed! Only God can see the possibilities each time we plant our seeds of faith. When we have Jesus' love on the inside, we have the power and the wisdom of God within us! That means we can produce lots of fruit! Fruit that will not only bless us, but also may reproduce God's love for others in ways that we can not even imagine. So what do we know about the fruit of the cacao pod? What's on the inside matters most! And what do we know about the life of the Christian? Say it with me: What's on the inside matters most! Excellent! I think you've earned your know chocolate award this Third Sunday in Lent.

[Hold up a package of chocolate-covered cacao or coffee beans.]

But first, let's talk to God together.

Dear God, Thank You for Jesus' love that fills us with Your goodness. Help us to share what Jesus gives us with the world. Amen.

[As the children are dismissed, distribute chocolate-covered cacao or coffee beans to each participant. Consider packaging a few pieces for each child in a small bag.]

Children's Messages
Fourth Sunday in Lent: Know When

Challenge

Know When
Know When it's time to share good news
Our Lenten commitment to "know chocolate" challenges us to share goodness with the world — both the recipes for chocolate delicacies and God's good news of Jesus Christ.

Chapter

John 3:14-21
Ephesians 2:1-10

Chart

Cacao beans ready for fermenting

Chocolate

Hot chocolate mix

Chat

From our last chat, we know which part of the cacao plant is the most important for making chocolate—the seeds found inside. In just the same way, for Christians we know what's on the inside matters most! When do you think people discovered the secret of turning a bitter little seed into something wonderful to taste? The known history of chocolate starts about the same time Jesus was born. The ancient Mayan people added cornmeal, Chile peppers, honey, and water to ground cacao seeds, then poured the mixture back and forth until it frothed. Everyone in Mayan culture enjoyed drinking chocolate. The Mayan priests even used a chocolate drink during special religious ceremonies. Later, when the Aztecs conquered the Mayans, chocolate became a special drink reserved only for the wealthy and powerful in Aztec society.

When the Spanish conquered the Aztec Empire, they brought the recipe for the Aztec chocolate drink to Europe. The Spanish added cinnamon and sugar, but kept their recipe a secret for another 100 years. When a Spanish princess married a French king, she gave his court the recipe as a wedding present. Soon the wealthy people across Europe were using special chocolate pots to serve the delicious drink. In fact, the saucer was invented to keep fancy ladies from dripping chocolate on their fine clothing. The drink was so popular among the royal courts that the Church allowed them to drink chocolate even during the season of Lent. However, ordinary people like us would not have been able to afford to buy chocolate to drink. When is it okay to keep something God-given a secret or to use God's gifts just for ourselves? Never! Chocolate is always for sharing, right? Say it with me: Chocolate is always for sharing.

Finally, in the early 1800s, a Dutch scientist named Coenraad Van Houten invented a machine called the chocolate press. This new invention allowed people to press the cocoa beans to make bars of chocolate and cocoa powder. This discovery meant chocolate could be stored easily and produced more cheaply. Then even common people could enjoy the delicious drink. At last, chocolate was available to everyone and all could share in its goodness. Is the message of Easter just for a chosen few? No! The Bible gives us God's recipe for hope—and it's no secret! John 3:16 tells us that God loves the world. Jesus died for everyone's sins and God raised Jesus on Easter morning so that the whole world could know God's power over sin and death. So if chocolate is always for sharing, what about God's love? God's love is always for sharing, too! Say it with me: God's love is always for sharing! Now you can share God's recipe for hope with the world. I think that deserves a know chocolate award, for sure! You can take this hot chocolate mix home to share.

[Hold up a packet of hot chocolate mix.]

But first, let's thank God together for sharing Jesus with us.

Dear God, Thank You for sending Jesus for the whole world. Help us to share Your recipe for hope with everyone who hungers and thirsts for it. Amen.

[As the children are dismissed, distribute a packet of hot chocolate mix to each participant.]

Children's Messages
Fifth Sunday in Lent: Know Why

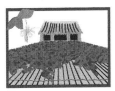

Challenge

Know Why
Know Why health benefits both body and soul
Our Lenten commitment to "know chocolate" challenges us to understand that God wants us to be healthy – both physically and spiritually.

Chapter

Luke 17:6-7
Hebrews 11:1-3

Chart

Dried cacao beans

Chocolate

Dark chocolate bars

Chat

From our last chat we know that both chocolate and God's love are always for sharing! We know God's love is good for us, but what about chocolate? It is true that there can be too much of a good thing, but the more scientists do research about chocolate, the more they discover the benefits chocolate can bring.

[Point to a picture of dried cacao beans.]

In order to make chocolate, the seeds of the cacao plant must be dried in the sun. Once they dry, the seeds' sticky covering turns a rich brown and becomes a hard outer shell. Now the seed is officially a cacao bean and ready to crush to release the inner chocolatey goodness. It is the inside of the cacao bean that holds the health benefits found in chocolate. Researchers tell us that the cacao bean is rich in flavonoids. These are compounds that contain antioxidants that are good for the body. They increase blood flow to the brain, work with our body's hormones to provide a sense of well being, and help reduce the build-up of plaque in the arteries which leads to better heart health. Studies also indicate that cocoa butter helps our bodies produce good cholesterol that offers protection from heart disease. Wow! Now we know why we like chocolate so much! Chocolate can be good for us!

There is something important to remember, however. The darker the chocolate we eat, the better it is for us. Dark chocolate contains more of the cacao bean and less sugar, milk fat, or other additives. However, because chocolate has a high fat content of its own, we still need to limit the amount of chocolate we eat. Some experts suggest that one ounce of dark chocolate per day is a good way to stay healthy. In fact, studies show that men who eat chocolate live on average a year longer than men who don't. So what do we want to remember? Chocolate is good for us! Say it with me: Chocolate is good for us!

Would you guess that faith is also proven to be good for us? You would guess correctly. Studies indicate that people who make faith, prayer, and Church attendance a priority have the same health advantages as people who exercise regularly and who don't smoke. I guess that just like more cacao in chocolate is healthy for us, the more God is a part of our lives the healthier we will be. Not only is chocolate good for us, faith is good for us! Say it with me: Faith is good for us! You've certainly earned your know chocolate award this week. It's a piece of dark chocolate—just like the doctor ordered! But first, let's thank God for giving us ways to be both physically and spiritually healthy!

Dear God, Thank You for the ways You provide to keep us healthy in body and in spirit. Amen.

[As the children are dismissed, distribute a piece of dark chocolate to each participant.]

Children's Messages
Sixth Sunday in Lent (Palm Sunday/Passion Sunday): Know So

Challenge

Know So
Know So choices can be based on wisdom
Our Lenten commitment to "know chocolate" challenges us to distinguish the genuine from the imitation – both in types of chocolates and in those we choose to follow.

Chapter

Matthew 21:1-11
Philippians 2:5-11

Chart

Crushed cacao beans

Chocolate

Chocolate mini-bars

Chat

In our last chat, we learned that chocolate is good for us just like faith is good for us! But the process of making chocolate has only just begun when the dried beans are sent to be roasted and crushed. Making high quality chocolate takes time. First the beans must be winnowed. Winnowing removes the hard outer shell of the bean and reveals the inner part called the nib. The nib is then crushed to extract the cocoa butter or oil from the bean. Then the cocoa butter and the crushed nibs are mixed together again to make chocolate.

[Point to picture of crushed cacao beans.]

Manufacturers can decide how much of the nibs remain in the cocoa butter to determine how dark the chocolate will be. Low quality chocolate is processed more quickly and can have many other ingredients added to it. The actual chocolate content of a product can be very low, or even non-existent. That is why we can not judge chocolate only with our eyes. We must read the ingredient list carefully and look for genuine chocolate. So we need to choose wisely! Say it with me: We need to choose wisely!

On this Palm Sunday we celebrate the story of Jesus coming into Jerusalem as God's Chosen, the Messiah. It seems strange to us that the people in the crowd on Palm Sunday would welcome Jesus as their king with a great parade, then later in the week demand that He be crucified. They didn't choose wisely. They thought Jesus was coming into Jerusalem to be their earthly king. The people hadn't read God's description carefully enough. God sent Jesus to rule in our hearts, not on a throne. On Palm Sunday we begin Holy Week—a time to remember why Jesus came and why He had to suffer death on a cross. Jesus accepted what happened to Him in the time we call Holy Week because He loves us. Jesus came to set us free from sin and death. Jesus came so we can choose salvation! What did we learn about chocolate? We must choose wisely! And when Jesus offers us salvation? Say it with me: We must choose wisely!

We are looking for God's genuine Messiah—not a cheap imitation. We are looking for a Savior! And we can read the story of Holy Week to really understand what that means. I think you are wise enough to choose your own know chocolate reward! But before we choose our favorite chocolate, let's choose to thank God for giving us Jesus as our Savior.

Dear God, Thank You for the power to choose. Help us to recognize the very best gift of all—Your Son, Jesus. Amen.

[As the children are dismissed, offer an assortment of chocolate mini-bars and invite each participant to choose one to take with her or him.]

Children's Messages
Maundy Thursday: Know By

Challenge

Know By
Know By remembering Jesus' words and deeds
Our Lenten commitment to "know chocolate" challenges us to remember those we love on special occasions – both with gifts of chocolate and with gifts of bread and cup.

Chapter

John 13:21-30
1 Corinthians 11:23-26

Chart

Advertisement for heart-shaped box of chocolates

Chocolate

Heart-shaped box of chocolates

Chat

In our last chat, we discovered that we need to read the ingredients and choose our chocolate wisely. In the same way, we need to read and understand God's reasons for sending Jesus so we can choose our Savior wisely, as well. We can know quality chocolate by reading the ingredients, but we also know what chocolate is best by the advertising that is all around us. Until the 1850s, chocolate was available only as a drink. Then some English folks named Cadbury discovered how to make a bar of chocolate. Later, some people in Switzerland named Nestle added milk to chocolate for a sweeter, smoother candy. So not much more than a hundred years ago, the first advertisements were created for boxes of chocolate to give as gifts to loved ones. The advertisements suggested that the person receiving the chocolate would fondly remember the one who gave such a delicious treat. In fact, the boxes in advertisements were shaped like a heart.

[Hold up the heart-shaped box of chocolates.]

That symbol suggests that chocolate is a gift worth remembering! Say it with me: Chocolate is a gift worth remembering!

During Holy Week, Maundy Thursday is about a gift worth remembering, as well. We celebrate the day when Jesus ate the Passover Meal with His disciples before He was arrested and crucified. Jesus told His followers that they should remember two symbols: the bread that He broke with them and the cup that He shared with them. The symbols were to remind them of His love every time they shared these elements in remembrance of Him. Today we still use the symbolic meal of bread and cup as a way to remember Christ's gift of sacrifice for us. Just like a heart-shaped box represents a loving remembrance, so do the symbols of bread and cup. If chocolate is a gift worth remembering, what can we say about the message of Maundy Thursday? Jesus is a Gift worth remembering! Say it with me: Jesus is a Gift worth remembering!

I think you are ready to receive your know chocolate award yet again! This time, we'll share from a heart-shaped box of chocolates as a reminder of God's great love that sent us God's own Son. But first, let's remember to be thankful for what Jesus did for us.

Dear God, We are grateful that You love us. We promise to remember what Jesus did to show us Your love. Amen.

[As the children are dismissed, allow each to select a piece of chocolate from the heart-shaped box of candy.]

Children's Messages
Good Friday: Know That

Challenge

Know That
Know That something bitter can make things better
Our Lenten commitment to "know chocolate" challenges us to accept that God can use what is bitter to produce something good – both in the taste of chocolate and in the life of Jesus.

Chapter

John 18:1-19:42
Hebrews 10:16-25

Chart

Symbol for fair trade chocolate

Chocolate

Fair trade chocolate

Chat

In our last chat, we recognized that—just as chocolate is a gift worth remembering—the message of Maundy Thursday is that Jesus is a gift worth remembering. If chocolate is that good, then why did the Aztecs call it *xocóatl* [sho-CO-lah-tul]—"bitter water"? Have you ever tasted baking chocolate or other chocolate that contains little or no sugar? If so, then you understand the use of the term bitter! Chocolate's unique flavor combines well with sweeteners to make a rich tasting treat — but without the added ingredients it would taste very bitter. The Aztecs did add vanilla and spices to their *xocóatl*, but the Spanish were the ones who made it sweet. Without that bitter under-taste, however, chocolate would not be as pleasing to our palates. In cooking, as well as in life, something bitter can make things better. Say it with me: Something bitter can make things better.

As we come to the Friday before Easter, this chocolate lesson can help us understand why we call this day "Good Friday." We might be tempted to think, "How can the day that Jesus died be called Good?" It certainly was not good for Jesus to be crucified. That was a bitter experience. The more we read and learn about the story of Good Friday, the more we understand what Jesus had to suffer. However, Jesus taught us on Maundy Thursday that His body and His blood were given so that we might have hope and new life. If Jesus did not experience death, then we would not know the joy of His resurrection on Easter morning. If Jesus did not offer Himself as a sacrifice for our sin, then we would not have the assurance of how much God loves us and is willing to forgive us. That makes the day of Jesus' death a Good Friday for each of us—we are saved, forgiven, and assured that we, too, will be raised to new life in eternity. Without Jesus' bitter experience, we would not appreciate God's sweet gift on Easter morning. Again we learn something bitter can make things better! Say it with me: Something bitter can make things better!

Chocolate, too, has gone through some tragic times. Because of people's love for chocolate and because it grew only near the equator, many countries made colonies of the chocolate-growing regions. That meant people growing the chocolate did not have control of their own country and often worked and slaved so that other people could enjoy chocolate delights. Today many chocolate farmers still make so little they can not afford to buy the chocolate they produce. But God can also use us to turn something bitter into something better. We can purchase fair trade chocolate and we can work to make sure big companies are paying fair prices for the chocolate they buy.

[Hold up a fair trade chocolate bar.]

Because Jesus made sacrifices for us, we can find the courage to make sacrifices to help make the world a better place for everyone—with God's help, we, too, can turn something bitter into something better. Say it with me: Turn something bitter into something better! Yes! We will share a fair trade know chocolate reward to remember the meaning of Good Friday. But first we should take time to talk to God together.

Dear God, Thank You for sending Jesus to give us hope that the bitter things of life can be made better. This Good Friday send us the strength to continue Your work in changing the world for the better. Amen.

[As the children are dismissed, distribute a piece of fair trade chocolate to each participant.]

Children's Messages
Easter Sunday: Know Who

Challenge

Know Who
Know Who calls us to follow in faith
Our Lenten commitment to "know chocolate" challenges us to learn the difference that can happen when we are open to change – just like the process that can make white chocolate or the miracle of resurrection that can make new life.

Chapter

John 20:1-18
1 Corinthians 15:1-11

Chart

Final product

Chocolate

White chocolate bunny, cross, egg, or lamb

Chat

Hallelujah! Christ is risen! Say it with me: Hallelujah! Christ is risen! He is risen, indeed! Say it with me: He is risen, indeed! That is the traditional Easter greeting among Christians around the world. The bitter news of Good Friday has turned into the sweet rejoicing of Easter morning. We have shared what it means to know chocolate for six long weeks of Lent, preparing for this special day. We have seen chocolate through all the stages of its growth, its harvesting, its processing, and its advertising. Now we can see the final product.

[Hold up a box of chocolate that contains at least one white chocolate piece or hold up the white chocolate bunny, cross, egg, or lamb.]

Wait a minute! When did chocolate turn white? I don't remember that part of the process, do you?

Actually, we did talk about crushing the cacao beans to separate the cocoa butter from the nibs. Then we said the manufacturers added as much of the crushed nibs back into the cocoa butter as they chose in order to make different levels of cacao flavor—from light to dark chocolate. We simply left out one option—not adding any of the nibs at all. If we add sugar and flavorings only to the separated cocoa butter, then we can have what people call "white chocolate." It certainly looks different, doesn't it?

Jesus looked different to the disciples after His resurrection, as well. When we read the story of the first Easter morning, we learn that Mary Magdalene thought Jesus was the gardener when she first encountered Him near the empty tomb. Jesus had been buried as a human being, but He was raised by God's power as our Messiah, our Savior. That must have been quite a transformation process—sort of like the crushing process that separates the dark outer part of the cocoa bean from the inner essence of cocoa butter. White chocolate can remind us that we have an inner essence, a spirit, as well.

The Easter story shows us that God offers us the gift of eternal life. The same resurrection power that raised Jesus from the dead will separate the outer shell of our physical bodies from our inner spirit—the part of us that God keeps alive. Just like in the Easter story, when Jesus calls Mary's name and she recognizes Him, Jesus calls our names, too. And when we understand Easter's message, we say: Hallelujah! Christ is risen! He is risen, indeed! Say it with me: Hallelujah! Christ is risen! He is risen, indeed! That is the most important know chocolate lesson of all! Your white chocolate award is waiting for you. But first, let's respond to God's call together.

Dear God, Thank You for raising Jesus to new life. We say yes to Christ's call to believe and follow Him. Amen.

[As the children are dismissed, distribute a piece of white chocolate to each participant.]

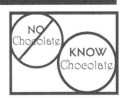

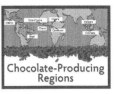

Chocolate-Producing Regions

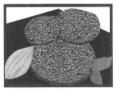

Lent and Easter

Calendars help to provide the structure for all aspects of our lives, and the Church is no exception. Just like the secular calendar reminds us of Valentine hearts or Thanksgiving turkeys, the Church calendar invites us to explore the story of salvation as we experience the festivals of faith. The Church Year coordinates the message of seven basic seasons—Advent, Christmas, Epiphany, Lent, Easter, Pentecost, and Ordinary Time—with slight variations among the denominations. Throughout this cycle we experience the life and ministry of Jesus, and the empowering of His Church to carry on the work God began in creation. Those stories become part of the rhythm of our lives—anticipated, celebrated, savored, and shared by all God's people. Rather than treasured fragments of disconnected text, the Bible becomes the woven fabric of a seamless garment, with each season flowing meaningfully to the next, completing the cycle, yet leading us to begin again the wonderful journey of faithful discipleship. To understand the focus and flavor of the Church Year during Lent and Easter, the following material provides an overview of each season.

Lent

Like Advent, Lent is a season of preparation. Historically in the Church, it was the time set aside for new converts to prepare for baptism or for backslidden Christians to do penance and be restored. The forty days prior to Easter were dedicated to fasting, prayer, and self-examination; however, Sundays were to be treated as "little Easters" when the fast and penance could be set aside to celebrate Jesus' victory. Hence, there are really forty-six days in Lent because Sundays are not counted.

Ash Wednesday marks the beginning of the time of preparation. In some Churches, last year's palms are burned and mixed with oil and the mixture placed on the foreheads of the faithful as a sign of humility. Some Churches designate a "Passion Sunday" one week before Easter to remember specifically the extreme suffering that Jesus experienced on the cross. The Sunday before Easter is also designated as "Palm Sunday" to commemorate Jesus' triumphant entry into Jerusalem and the beginning of "Holy Week" with the events that led up to the crucifixion. Maundy Thursday calls for a celebration of the institution of the Sacrament of Communion that stems from the Passover Seder Jesus shared with His disciples. "Good Friday" is a paradoxical celebration of Jesus' death: while the suffering of crucifixion can hardly be called "good," the atonement for sin and the gift of salvation through Christ's sacrifice is "good news" for the Christian. The waiting of Lent is finally over with the arrival of Easter Sunday and the joy of Resurrection.

Scriptures studied during Lent present the forty days of Jesus' wandering in the desert after His baptism, being tested, and preparing for ministry. During this time as well, the Church reads the Transfiguration story, accounts of Jesus' encounters with religious leaders, and passages that relate Jesus' awareness of His mission and its consequences. The Christian's challenge to spend forty days in reflection and spiritual discipline seems to parallel the message of the season.

The color for Lent is again purple, a color reminding us of the darkness of our sin and the royalty of Jesus. On Good Friday the color is sometimes changed to black until Easter Sunday to symbolize mourning. Often an early sunrise service marks the transition from darkness to light, replacing black with white.

Easter

The season of Easter begins with the Sunday of the celebration of the resurrection, which changes each year based on the cycles of the moon. Easter Sunday is the first Sunday after the first full moon after the vernal equinox that occurs around March 21. So Easter can be as early as March 22 and as late as April 25. Some scholars say the day for Easter was set to assure the light of the moon for pilgrims traveling to Jerusalem. Obviously, the first Easter was established based on the Jewish celebration of the Passover. The Orthodox Churches continue to use Passover as the determining date for Easter services with their Palm Sunday occurring the first Sunday after Passover begins.

On the first Easter morning, God made a difference for human beings forever. God raised Jesus from death to new life. Easter is a season of hope that invites God's people to rejoice that because Jesus lives, we, too, will live—

eternally. Easter reminds us that we can experience God's renewal now and forever when we believe in Christ's resurrection.

Easter is more than a special day in the Church Year. It is actually a season of fifty days in which we celebrate the joy of the new day Christ's resurrection brings to the world. But even more, as we proclaim God's plan of hope and salvation for all people, we discover that Easter is a way of life. During the season of Easter, Christians celebrate the resurrection and tell the stories of Jesus' appearances to the disciples. Ascension Day occurs during this season, forty days after Easter Sunday, and celebrates Jesus' return to Heaven to reign at the right hand of God. The promise of the gift of the Spirit and the challenge to "go into all the world" are a part of the Easter season as well.

The color for Easter is white, the color reserved for the holiest festivals of the Church Year.

Learning Activities
Adult Study Overview

The Adult Study for the congregational resource *Know Chocolate for Lent* owes a debt of gratitude to Hilary Brand's books for exploring the film *Chocolat*, both *Christ and the Chocolaterie: A Lent Course* (London: Darton, Longman, & Todd, 2002) and *Chocolate for Lent: A Creative Approach to Your Lenten Journey* (Boston: Pauline Books & Media, 2004). While complementary to these two works, the attempt in the Adult Study for *Know Chocolate for Lent* is to offer a simple protocol for thinking about the film, the Church, the Season, and ourselves. Discussion leaders may find useful information by reading the other titles; however, adults can participate in conversation and offer reflections throughout the study based solely on the Scripture passages, the film, the handouts, and their own experience. Those who wish a more in-depth look at the film for Lenten study would be well advised to consult Brand's reflections, background, and questions developed for that purpose.

Leaders can set up the *Know Chocolate for Lent* Adult Study series in a variety of ways: as a discussion class for the six Sundays of Lent, as a mid-week series throughout the season, or as a course any time adults wish to focus on the nature of the Church and the application of Christian discipleship. The six handouts can be duplicated and used to guide discussion following a similar protocol for each gathering: reading the Scripture(s), viewing selected clips from the film, asking questions to spur discussion, and applying what is learned to today's Christian experience. Participants are encouraged to apply what they have learned in the week between each study session. After the first week, the leader should begin by asking group members to share any observations or insights that they gained since the last session.

Obviously, group members benefit by a working knowledge of the complete film, *Chocolat*, so it is desirable to arrange a screening or encourage the participants to view the movie in its entirety prior to the study. Leaders should secure a license to show the film if it is done in a group setting.

Film studies are wonderful opportunities for adults to explore and to share their thoughts and reflections with their peers. Encouraging everyone to learn to pay attention to the way director's frame shots; the subtlety of camera angles, focus, and movement; the importance of transitions between moments or characters; and other cinematography techniques will enhance the viewers' enjoyment and appreciation of every film.

Viewing Guide for *Chocolat*

Chocolat may seem an odd film to study for Lent. First and foremost the story presents its more religious figures in a rather negative light—as people who live very fearful, unhappy, restricted lives. The more colorful (literally), attractive characters appear to resist moral codes and to be more tolerant, more loving, and more intelligent. What kind of film is this for Christians to study? However, keep an open mind until the end of the film and then reflect on the message we may find as we consider who we are and who God calls us to be as faithful followers of the Gospel.

Suggestions

Notice the physical setting of the film and how those details affect the story—

> The tight-knit community
> The dominance of the church
> The wind
> The river

Notice the use of color—

> The backdrop of drab grays
> The vividness of Vianne's and others' clothing

Consider the symbolism—

> The wind, the river, and the colors
> The imaginary kangaroo with the bad leg
> The exotic décor from South America
> And, of course, the Chocolate!

The List of *Chocolat's* main characters

Vianne	The journeying chocolate maker; daughter of Chitza and George
Anouk	Vianne's daughter
Comte de Reynaud	The Mayor of Lasquenet
Roux	The "river rat"
Armande Voizin	Old lady with diabetes, Caroline's mother
Caroline Clairmont	Daughter of Armande, mother to Luc, secretary to the Comte
Serge Muscat	Drunken café owner
Josephine Muscat	Serge's battered wife
Guillaume Blerot	Retired gentleman with dog, Charlie
Madame Audel	Widow to whom Guillaume is attracted
Père Henri	Priest
Yvette Marceau	Wife starving for physical affection
Alphonse Marceau	Weary husband

Adult Study
Week One: Knowing What to Give Up

Read

Matthew 4:1-11, 18-22
Mark 10:17-27

View

Comte in his study, refusing food
Josephine going into the chocolaterie
Guillaume meeting the three widows

To Get Started Thinking

- Why do you think Lent has become a season for giving up our favorite foods?
- What do the Scriptures seem to suggest?
- What does the film seem to suggest?

Application

Make a quick list of all the things you can think of that might be beneficial to give up, whether for a short while or for good.

Things to give up	Reasons this would be beneficial

Chocolat is superficially about a battle between self-denial—giving up food—and self-indulgence—enjoying chocolate. But what other self-indulgent behaviors could the villagers give up? What self-denying behaviors could Vianne stand to give up? How do those ideas compare to our list above?

To Take with Us into the Week

- Ask God to show us what we really need to give up and what foolish sacrifices we are making.
- Remember that we need to receive God's grace for the journey of Lent—enough for ourselves and enough to share with each other.

Adult Study
Week Two: Knowing How to Give

Read

Luke 14:1-24
Romans 12:13
1 Peter 4:9
Hebrews 13:2
John 2:1-11

View

Armande reminiscing
Vianne's gift to Josephine
Vianne visiting Josephine
Armande's party

To Get Started Thinking

- To what extent is Christianity a way of life that is based on keeping the rules? What rules did Jesus seem to follow?
- What do the Scriptures seem to suggest?
- What does the film seem to suggest?

Application

How does the main character Vianne interact with her community? How is she different than the villagers? Is she tempting people to take what they want or helping them to discover what they need? Why do you think so? Do Vianne's choices represent a Christian lifestyle? Why or why not?

Choices Vianne makes	Christian Principles Represented

Chocolat is superficially about a battle between holding a moral standard—keeping the rules—and practicing tolerance—welcoming those who are "different." To what extent is Christianity both a moral code and a welcoming lifestyle?

To Take with Us into the Week

- Ask God to show us where we need to keep the boundaries clear and when we need to be more tolerant and hospitable.
- Remember that we need to receive God's grace for the journey of Lent — enough for ourselves and enough to share with each other.

Adult Study
Week Three: Knowing Whom We Worship

Read

Matthew 12:1-21

View

Opening scene in Church, winds blow door, Vianne's arrival
Widows looking in shop window to Comte talking with Pere Henri

To Get Started Thinking

- To what extent is the Church about tradition?
- What do the Scriptures seem to suggest?
- What does the film seem to suggest?
- What is helpful about tradition? What is hurtful? What would Jesus say?

Application

In the film, who are the "controllers" and who are the "controlled"?
How is authority acquired? How is authority misused?
Who are the defiant ones? How do they stand up to those who intimidate?
How does the film's view of "spiritual authority" apply to the Church today?

Controllers	The Controlled	Methods Used to Intimidate or Rebel

Chocolat is essentially about the dangers of spiritual authority—intolerance and intimidation by those in control—versus the authentic life of the Spirit. How does the Church find a way to be a force for God in the world without resorting to coercion?

To Take with Us into the Week

- Ask God to show us how to relinquish the need to dominate and control the world by releasing ourselves to God's dominion and becoming a Christ-like servant.
- Remember that we need to receive God's grace for the journey of Lent—enough for ourselves and enough to share with each other.

Adult Study
Week Four: Knowing without Judging

Read

John 4:4-26
Mark 12:28-31

View

Vianne and Armande in the chocolaterie
Vianne meeting Roux
Serge apologizing to Josephine
The public meeting

To Get Started Thinking

- When you meet someone whose belief systems or traditions are different than your own, do you first notice similarities or differences? Why?
- What does the Scripture seem to suggest?
- What does the film seem to suggest?
- What is more important being or doing? What would Jesus say?

Application

In the film, who are those more concerned with being? Who are those more concerned with doing?

Being	Doing

Chocolat is essentially about the dangers of prejudice and self-righteousness and about the importance of confessing and forgiving. How do we best extend welcome and preach the Good News?

To Take with Us into the Week

- Ask God to show us how to balance both being and doing so that we can more fully forgive and more fully share love.
- Remember that we need to receive God's grace for the journey of Lent—enough for ourselves and enough to share with each other.

Adult Study
Week Five: Knowing How to Receive

Read

John 3:1-8
Matthew 18:1-3

View

Caroline mends the bike
Armande's funeral
Vianne drawn by her mother's ashes
Caroline and Comte, "No one would think less of you. . . ."

To Get Started Thinking

- Think about a time in which you grew the most in responsibility, in courage, in spiritual stature – or any "rebirth" which took you to a new level of living. What precipitated that change — strength or weakness?
- What has to be left behind in order for us to be "reborn"?
- What does the Scripture seem to suggest?
- What does the film seem to suggest?

Application

In the film, which characters choose to grow up? What changes did they have to acknowledge in order to do so? What controlling influences did they have to leave behind?

Character	Change	Initiating Event	Resulting Event	Controlling Influence Left behind
Caroline				
Luc				
Josephine				
Comte				
Pere Henri				
Vianne				

Chocolat emphasizes the humanity rather than the divinity of Christ. Which do you think our Church emphasizes? What difference would it make if we shifted the balance? What are the dangers of emphasizing one over the other? How do we find a balance?

To Take with Us into the Week

- Ask God to show us how to acknowledge our failures and embrace our need for grace in order to be more fully human and alive. Change is obligatory; transformation is optional.
- Remember that we need to receive God's grace for the journey of Lent – enough for ourselves and enough to share with each other.

Adult Study
Week Six: Knowing Whom We Follow

Read

> Ecclesiastes 3:1
> Luke 4:18
> Matthew 7:24-27

View

> Comte's chocolate excesses
> Pere Henri's Easter sermon
> The chocolate festival
> Vianne throws out ashes

To Get Started Thinking

- How has the film demonstrated the very mission that Jesus proclaimed God had given Him?
- What Christian symbolism did you notice in the chocolate festival?
- What reflections can you share about how studying the film has supported our study of Scripture and Lenten themes?
- What have we learned is the sacrifice that pleases God?

Application

In the film, which characters best represent positive Christian principles to you? What did they say or do to communicate that message? What does that tell us about how we share our belief during Lent and throughout the rest of the year?

Character	Christian Principle Observed	Based on which specific action or speech?	Application to sharing my beliefs
Caroline			
Luc			
Josephine			
Comte			
Pere Henri			
Vianne			
Armande			

Chocolat seems to propose a generous tolerance more than a specific belief system. What are the pros and cons of de-emphasizing doctrines? How can a denomination or congregation survive if its members emphasize tolerance over common beliefs?

To Take with Us into the Week

- Ask God to show us how to deepen our own beliefs while becoming more tolerant of others.
- Remember that we need to receive God's grace for the journey of Lent – enough for ourselves and enough to share with each other.

Children's Programs

While using the children's sermon series from *Know Chocolate for Lent*, found in the Worship section of this resource, enrich the students' experiences by offering any of the following activities in Sunday and mid-week programs.

Architecture

- Discover the impact of the rise of "Chocolate Houses" in Europe during the 1700s. Discuss the difference between Central American design and European design for gathering places and the use of chocolate in celebrations.
- Research ancient Mayan civilization to discover the culture that gave rise to the enjoyment of chocolate.

Art

- Make a collage of candy wrappers to represent some phrase associated with chocolate: for example, spell out the words "Fair Trade," "God's Gift," or "Save the Rainforest!"
- Visit a pottery-design shop and decorate a "chocolate pot."

Banners/Textiles

- Create the banner as suggested in the Enhancements section of this resource.
- Design a "Know Chocolate" T-shirt with fabric paint.

Creative Writing

- Create an acrostic for the word C-H-O-C-O-L-A-T-E to express thanksgiving for God's good gifts.
- Write a letter to a fair-trade chocolate company such as Divine Chocolate, 1730 Connecticut Ave NW, 2nd Floor, Washington, DC 20009. Thank them for their commitment to help farmers receive fair wages for their work.

Culinary

- Do a "chocolate tour" of the local community. Visit bakeries, candy shops, or restaurants to taste chocolate treats. Consider creating a one to five star rating of the recipes or concoctions available and write a "chocolate tour review."
- Research the ancient Aztec recipes for preparing chocolate to drink. Learn about the different tools used and the methods followed. Attempt to re-create an Aztec hot chocolate drink, complete with Chile peppers.

Dance

- Find a recording of music from Central America or other chocolate-growing regions of the world. For example, *Music from the Chocolate Lands*, Putumayo, 2004. Encourage the children to choreograph their own moves to the sounds.
- Watch the dance scene from Armande's birthday party in the film *Chocolat*. Invite the participants to dance along.

Drama

- Ask the students to imagine what it is like to be a farmer in Central America or Africa. Have them act out the motions involved in harvesting cacao in the equatorial rainforest.
- Involve the participants in improvisational theater based on the history of chocolate. Practice facial expressions and non-verbal body language and then give small groups a situation to enact. For example, one scenario might be Montezuma offering chocolate to drink to the first Spanish visitors.

Games

- Play a game of Charades using terms and situations related to the growing of chocolate, for example: midge fly, cacao plant, or chocolate pot.
- Set up a Concentration game using the words and symbols from each week's children's message.

Music

- Listen to recordings of rainforest sounds. Invite the students to try to recreate the sounds they hear.
- Make "rainforest music" with rain sticks and other African instruments.

Photography

- Find pictures in books that demonstrate the stages of growth of the cacao plant. Note the sequence and changes the pictures depict.
- Look in books, magazines, and on Internet sites to find images of advertising posters for chocolate. If possible, trace how the images and representations have changed through the years.

Puppetry

- Construct a cacao plant puppet to tell the story of how chocolate grows.
- Make a family of puppets out of craft sticks to represent the workers on a chocolate farm. Have each age and gender represented and explain the role each person plays in making the family farm successful.

Storytelling

- Invite readers to discuss the differences between the book by Roald Dahl *Charlie and the Chocolate Factory* and any of the *Willy Wonka* films.
- Read the book *Harvest of Hope* and discuss what surprises the listeners about the chocolate growing process.

Women's Retreat
A Chocolate Feast: Celebrating God's Goodness
Overview

The Adult Study, found in the Education section of the book *Know Chocolate for Lent: A Resource for Congregations*, can be used to design a Women's Retreat called "A Chocolate Feast: Celebrating God's Goodness" for a day, an overnight, or an entire weekend. The outline provided assumes a weekend setting; however, leaders can easily omit or condense parts to fit the time frame available. In any setting, it also includes a closing worship experience.

Designing a Weekend Retreat: Suggested Schedule

Friday Evening

> Dinner
> Viewing the film *Chocolat*
> Discussion using the handout for Week One of the Adult Study
> Evening Prayer

Saturday Morning

> Breakfast
> Morning Devotions
> Group Building Activities
> Discussion using the handout for Week Two of the Adult Study

Saturday Afternoon

> Lunch
> Group Building Activities
> Discussion using the handouts for Week Three and Week Four of the Adult Study
> Free time

Saturday Evening

> Dinner
> Group Building Activities
> Discussion using the handouts for Week Five and Week Six of the Adult Study
> Evening Prayer

Sunday Morning

> Breakfast
> Group Sharing of Important Learning
> Chocolate Feast

Creating the Environment: Suggested Surroundings

- Burn candles with chocolate fragrance.
- Make a collage of chocolate wrappers opened during the weekend as a wall mural.
- Play recordings that include sounds of the rainforest or music from the chocolate lands.
- Provide ample opportunities for sampling chocolate—mini candy bars, foil-covered kisses, special dark chocolates, or any favorite chocolate brands.
- Set up a worship area with a chocolate-related theme. Consider using a chocolate fountain, chocolate-themed decorations and dishes, and pictures or posters about the chocolate-growing process.
- Use green plants, props, and posters to create a rainforest feel to the gathering place.

Enhancing the Experience: Suggested Group Building Activities

- Develop games based on the theme of chocolate; for example create a Chocolate Trivia game to play or play a Pictionary game using phrases that contain the word chocolate.
- Divide the timeline of chocolate history into segments and ask the group to race against a time limit to put the information in the correct sequence.
- Invite the participants to share their favorite chocolate temptation and a memory connected to the treat.
- Look at pictures of the chocolate-growing process and share facts about chocolate and its history.
- Make up piggyback songs about Lent, Chocolate, or Faith based on familiar tunes.
- Provide paper and a saddle stapler and ask the group to make journals by folding 8 ½" x 11" paper in half and stapling it in the middle. Provide magazines, newspaper advertisements, and stickers—as well as scissors, markers, and glue—so that the participants can personalize their journals. Challenge the participants to write their reflections, questions, and prayers on the pages they create.

Extending the Experience: Suggested Options

- Bring artifacts from the retreat such as the container of M&M'S® from the chocolate feast, newsprint lists of insights or suggestions for ways to grow the Church, or decorations used to suggest the chocolate or rainforest theme.
- Take pictures throughout the weekend and build a visual presentation to show during a fellowship time.

Women's Retreat
A Chocolate Feast: Celebrating God's Goodness
Worship Preparation

As a closing worship experience of a *Know Chocolate for Lent* Women's Retreat, celebrate God's goodness with a chocolate feast.

Items needed for the celebration include:

Baskets and bowls
Bibles
Candy for each participant:

- Dove Chocolate
- Hershey's Kisses, 2 per person
- M&M'S®, individual packet
- Milk Duds, mini-box
- Milky Way
- Mounds
- Pretzel twist, small chocolate-covered

Chocolate and items for dipping in chocolate fountain such as fruit, marshmallows, pound cake, and pretzels
Chocolate fountain
Communion cups, disposable
Copy machine
Equipment for Aztec chocolate drink

- Baster
- Blender (Optional)
- Grater
- Measuring cups and spoons
- Microwave or stove
- Mixing bowl
- Whisk

Forks
Gift bags for chocolate items, 1 per person
Handouts/Scripts for Chocolate Feast: Leader, Participants, Readers
Ingredients for Aztec chocolate drink recipe

- Chile peppers or cayenne pepper, ground
- Dark baking chocolate or dark cocoa powder
- Vanilla
- Water

Music for selected songs

- "Amazing Grace"
- "Here I Am, Lord"
- " I Will Call Upon the Lord"
- "Lord, Be Glorified"
- "Seek Ye First"
- "Spirit of the Living God"
- "This Is the Day"

Napkins
Paper, 8 ½" x 11"
Plates
Table
Tablecloth
Vase or glass container

Advance Preparation

Make an Aztec chocolate drink to place in an individual communion cup for each participant.

- 1 ounce unsweetened dark baking chocolate or 2 Tablespoons dark cocoa powder
- 1 teaspoon vanilla
- 2/3 cup boiling water
- Ground Chile pepper to taste

If using dark baking chocolate, grate it into a bowl and add just enough boiling water to melt the chocolate and make a paste. If using the dark cocoa powder mix with equal parts water and stir to make a paste. Then add the rest of the water and the vanilla. Stir with a whisk until the mixture is well blended or use a blender, if available. Add ground Chile peppers to taste—just enough to give a little kick. Increase proportions of ingredients to make enough to fill the necessary communion cups 2/3 full. Use a baster to fill each disposable communion cup with the drink.

Place each type of candy used in the Chocolate Feast in a small basket or bowl and arrange them around the chocolate fountain. Assign someone to distribute the candies as a part of the celebration or plan to pass each type of chocolate around at the appropriate time in the service.

Set up the chocolate fountain and prepare the items that will be dipped in it. Arrange plates, napkins, and forks on the table.

Recruit seven participants who will each share one Scripture reading at the beginning of each segment of the celebration.

Women's Retreat
A Chocolate Feast: Celebrating God's Goodness
Worship Leader's Script

[As people gather for the Chocolate Feast, distribute a small package of M&M'S® to each person. Tell the participants that they will pour the colorful candies into the glass container on the worship center as a part of the Call to Worship.]

Gather—M&M'S®—Make Merry before the Lord!

Leader

As we gather, let us pour out our hearts before the Lord.

[Invite the participants to begin emptying their M&M'S® into the glass container. Ask the participants to give thanks silently for the gift of life as each pours her candy. Give a signal when it is time for the women to return to their seats.]

Just as these multi-colored candies gather in this vase, we — God's people — in all our diversity gather in this place to worship. And God receives us, different as we are. Listen to these words of Scripture.

Reader One—Psalm 62:8

"Pour out your hearts to him, for God is our refuge."

Leader

Refuge means "Shelter" — God is our sanctuary, our shelter, our refuge — much like the rainforest provides the shelter so the cacao tree can grow. We rejoice in God's sheltering love.

Sing

"This Is the Day"

Offer "Mounds" of Praise—God is Indescribably Delicious

Leader

As we offer our "mounds" of praise, let us remember how indescribable is the goodness of the God we serve.

[Distribute the Mounds bars around the group.]

As you think of the mounds of words you might use to describe God's goodness, listen to the Psalmist who offers us these words.

Reader Two—Psalm 34:8

"Taste and see that the Lord is good; blessed is the one who takes refuge in him."

Leader

The proof is in the taste—we know God's goodness by our experience and we boldly tell others about the goodness that we know! Just as we know that chocolate tastes richer as the percent of cacao increases, so our testimony to the world becomes richer the more we invite God to be part of our lives. God is here with us! God is pure goodness! Yet God waits for us to call in response to God's invitation to share in that goodness. If you would invite God into life, then sing together!

Sing

"I Will Call Upon the Lord"

Confess—The "Duds" of Life

Leader

God calls to us and we respond. But finding ourselves in the presence of pure goodness makes us all too aware of our own imperfections, our "duds" in life — sticky at the center. How did we dare to be so bold as to respond to One we are not worthy to approach?

[Pass around the Milk Duds as the symbol of our own "sticky centers."]

But Jesus came to assure us that we are loved and welcomed, that we can be forgiven in His name. Listen to these words from Scripture.

Reader Three—1 John 1:9

"If we confess our sins, he is faithful and just and will forgive us our sins and purify us from all unrighteousness."

Leader

Our "goodness" is just a sweet veneer—hiding the sticky center that possesses us. Yet, the sticky center of the cacao bean becomes the bittersweet source for chocolate. The bitterness of our own sin contrasts sweetly with God's amazing grace! Receive God's assurance of complete forgiveness as we sing.

Sing

"Amazing Grace"

Receive—A "Milky Way" of Blessings

Leader

In God's grace we are invited into relationship with the Creator of the Universe who goes by many names. The "Milky Way" is God's creation; the candy bar of the same name is a human creation. Yet, the name of the candy bar is actually not the one intended. The wrappers for the "Milky Way" were accidentally used for the candy known as "Three Musketeers" and vice-versa. If you think about the two bars, the "Three Musketeers" has a milky center and the "Milky Way" is made of three components—chocolate, caramel, and nougat. However, once the mistake was made, the promoters thought it was too costly to correct it, so the two new candy bars were introduced with names opposite of those intended. No matter their names, however, the candy is just as sweet. So it is with God—we experience the goodness of God's blessing and recognize the source, no matter what name people use to describe that goodness. Listen to this reminder from Scripture.

Reader Four—John 1:16

"From the fullness of his grace we have all received one blessing after another."

Leader

Do you know the scientific name for chocolate? "Theobromine"—food of the gods. Whatever name we use for God—it must mean "Yes!" to love. That love is the essence of Who God is and what God does. Experiencing that love is the goal of those who long for God's kingdom. Sing together a reminder of the intent of our seeking.

Sing

"Seek Ye First"

Respond—With a Holy "Kiss"

Leader

What we seek for ourselves we must be willing to share with others. We can not just take the sweet things of life to enjoy and forget those who hunger and thirst around us. Listen to the challenge from the writer of the book of Hebrews.

Reader Five — Hebrews 13:16

"And do not forget to do good and to share with others, for with such sacrifices God is pleased."

Leader

Our actions for God speak louder than our words to God. When we understand that faith is love in action, then we know that God invites us into relationship so that we have what we need to bring God's love to earth in our own lives.

[Distribute the chocolate kisses—two each, one to enjoy and one to share.]

We used to know only chocolate's sweetness. Now that we know chocolate better, we understand the importance of standing up for the right use of our world's resources and its people's lives. We cannot just eat and be satisfied. We must eat and be strengthened to do battle for what is right—what is loving. This chocolate is called a kiss because of the sound it makes when the machine places the chocolate on the conveyor belt. So Christians should be named because the love we share imitates that of Christ. Let us offer our lives as a sacrifice to God so that God's ways may be glorified on earth.

Sing

"Lord, Be Glorified"

Chocolate Celebration

Leader

While communion most often uses traditional elements of bread and grape juice, today we share a celebration in a non-traditional way. The bread is baked in pretzel shape—a shape first invented by monks as a children's snack for Lent, reminding them to say their prayers, hands folded across their chests. The cup holds a chocolate drink reminiscent of the early Aztec recipes—bitter and sweet—reminding us that God's grace atones for the bitterness of sin through the sacrifice of Jesus. As we receive these symbols, may they remind us again that in Jesus, God makes all things new!

[Distribute and share the chocolate-covered pretzels and the chocolate drink.]

Pray

Lord, we marvel at the ways you use the most humble plants in miraculous ways to provide us with an enjoyable feast. We marvel even more that You can use us to bring Your Goodness to the world.

Sing

"Spirit of the Living God"

Take Flight—On the Wings of a "Dove"

Leader

We have gathered to praise, receive, and respond to God's goodness. Now God provides us with the energy we need to live in a world that is broken and needs God's healing. Listen to the words that Jesus told His disciples.

Reader Six—John 14:26

"But the Counselor, the Holy Spirit, whom the Father will send in my name, will teach you all things and will remind you of everything I have said to you."

Reader Seven—John 20:22

And with that he breathed on them and said, "Receive the Holy Spirit."

Leader

God gives you the comfort of the Holy Spirit.

[Distribute the Dove Chocolate.]

You are prepared now to share the Good News! Remember, God's "Yes!" to love is for everyone. Once chocolate was just for the chosen few. There are still those for whom such a blessing is out of reach. We must work to make the world better for those who have too little goodness in their lives. God's love is not just for the chosen few. Yet there are those who don't even know God's blessing in their lives. We have been the "chosen few" too long. Now we must work to share God's Good News with the world! If you would be one whom God could send to those who do not know God's voice, then offer your lives in song.

Sing

"Here I Am, Lord"

Leader

You have been filled with God's goodness. Now you are ready to go and share with everyone what God brings into your life. Go in peace. God's goodness goes with you to sustain, inspire, and empower you to be the difference the world needs.

[Invite the participants to enjoy the chocolate feast prepared around the table.]

Women's Retreat
A Chocolate Feast: Celebrating God's Goodness
Worship Participant's Guide

Gather—M&M'S®—Make Merry before the Lord!

Reader One—Psalm 62:8

"Pour out your hearts to him, for God is our refuge."

Sing

"This Is the Day"

Offer "Mounds" of Praise—God Is Indescribably Delicious

Reader Two—Psalm 34:8

"Taste and see that the Lord is good; blessed is the one who takes refuge in him."

Sing

"I Will Call Upon the Lord"

Confess—The "Duds" of Life

Reader Three—1 John 1:9

"If we confess our sins, he is faithful and just and will forgive us our sins and purify us from all unrighteousness."

Sing

"Amazing Grace"

Receive—A "Milky Way" of Blessings

Reader Four—John 1:16

"From the fullness of his grace we have all received one blessing after another."

Sing

"Seek Ye First"

Respond—With a Holy "Kiss"

Reader Five—Hebrews 13:16

"And do not forget to do good and to share with others, for with such sacrifices God is pleased."

Sing

"Lord, Be Glorified"

Chocolate Celebration

Sing

"Spirit of the Living God"

Take Flight—On the Wings of a "Dove"

Reader Six—John 14:26

"But the Counselor, the Holy Spirit, whom the Father will send in my name, will teach you all things and will remind you of everything I have said to you."

Reader Seven—John 20:22

"And with that he breathed on them and said, 'Receive the Holy Spirit.'"

Sing

"Here I Am, Lord"

Women's Retreat
A Chocolate Feast: Celebrating God's Goodness
Worship Reader's Scripture Selections

Reader One—Psalm 62:8

"Pour out your hearts to him, for God is our refuge."

Reader Two—Psalm 34:8

"Taste and see that the Lord is good; blessed is the one who takes refuge in him."

Reader Three—1 John 1:9

"If we confess our sins, he is faithful and just and will forgive us our sins and purify us from all unrighteousness."

Reader Four—John 1:16

"From the fullness of his grace we have all received one blessing after another."

Reader Five—Hebrews 13:16

"And do not forget to do good and to share with others, for with such sacrifices God is pleased."

Reader Six—John 14:26

"But the Counselor, the Holy Spirit, whom the Father will send in my name, will teach you all things and will remind you of everything I have said to you."

Reader Seven—John 20:22

"And with that he breathed on them and said, 'Receive the Holy Spirit.'"

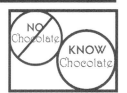

Overview

Family Devotions

Ash Wednesday: Know What

First Sunday in Lent: Know Where

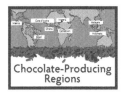

Chocolate-Producing Regions

Second Sunday in Lent: Know How

Third Sunday in Lent: Know Which

Fourth Sunday in Lent: Know When

Fifth Sunday in Lent: Know Why

Sixth Sunday in Lent (Palm Sunday/Passion Sunday): Know So

Maundy Thursday: Know By

Good Friday: Know That

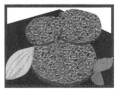

Easter Sunday: Know Who

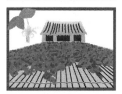

Overview

Know Chocolate for Lent offers a thematic approach for communicating the message of the Lent and Easter seasons of the Church Year. *Know Chocolate for Lent* uses the growing and manufacturing process of chocolate as a metaphor for the growth of faith and discipleship in the Christian life.

Know Chocolate for Lent invites families to share in the preparation for Easter by using a series of Lenten devotions at home as the focus for weekly activities. Family worship suggestions are provided for devotions including Scripture, story, and prayer. Six ideas for living out the message complete each week's preparation, building toward Easter Sunday and the resurrection of Jesus Christ.

The family devotions for *Know Chocolate for Lent* include showing a weekly symbol to represent the theme. Families could copy the illustrations in the Enhancements section of this resource to display as visual aids.

Know Chocolate for Lent challenges family members to use Lent as an opportunity to experience the goodness of God's gifts—both the gift of chocolate and the gift of new life.

Family Devotions
Ash Wednesday: Know What

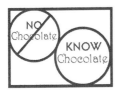

Read

Matthew 6:1-6, 16-21
2 Corinthians 5:20b-6:10

Say

Know What
Know What we often take for granted
Our Lenten commitment to "know chocolate" challenges us to recognize that we often take life's best gifts for granted – whether it is chocolate or God's loving presence.

Show

NO Chocolate/KNOW Chocolate Poster
Wrappers from chocolate products

Say

It looks like there is NO chocolate in any of these wrappers!

[Hold up the empty chocolate wrappers.]

Today is Ash Wednesday, the first day of the forty-day season called Lent. Sometimes during Lent we hear people say that they plan to give up chocolate for the forty days until Easter arrives. Giving up something we find tempting – especially chocolate – is one way to better understand the sacrifice Jesus made for us. This Lent, instead of NO – N-O—chocolate for Lent, we will KNOW – K-N-O-W—chocolate for Lent. We will learn where chocolate grows and who works hard so that we can have a chocolate bar whenever we want. If we know chocolate, then we will not eat our favorite candy without thinking about who makes chocolate possible. Without the season of Lent, we might just enjoy Easter but never understand the story of Jesus' life, death, and resurrection. On Ash Wednesday, these empty wrappers can remind us that today we begin a journey toward an empty tomb.

Pray

Dear God, Help us to know that all good things come from You. During Lent, may we empty our lives to be filled by Your goodness. Amen.

Taste

Chocolate kisses

Do This Week

Bake cookies with a chocolate kiss center to share with others.

Create a bumper sticker on self-adhesive backed paper with the play on words: NO Jesus, NO Peace; KNOW Jesus, KNOW Peace.

Draw pictures to show the ways Jesus suggests that we honor God by giving to the needy, fasting, and sharing our treasure (Matthew 6:1-6, 16-21).

Make a collage of empty chocolate wrappers with a title KNOW Chocolate for Lent!

Visit a library, bookstore, or Internet sites to see what information is available about the history and manufacturing process surrounding the chocolate industry.

Write a piggyback song to a simple tune about enjoying chocolate during Lent. For example, to "Row, Row, Row Your Boat" sing the words: Know, know, know your chocolate for forty days of Lent, then you'll know how good God is and why Jesus was sent.

Family Devotions
First Sunday in Lent: Know Where

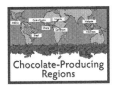

Chocolate-Producing Regions

Read

Mark 1:9-15
1 Peter 3:18-22

Say

Know Where
Know Where the best growth occurs
Our Lenten commitment to "know chocolate" challenges us to acknowledge God's plan for providing growing conditions—both in the rainforest and in the Church.

Show

World Map depicting chocolate-producing regions

Say

We begin our Lenten journey by discovering where chocolate grows. Chocolate bars are not picked from bushes! But chocolate does begin by growing on a tree, called the cacao [kah-COW] tree. The cacao tree can only develop within twenty degrees of the equator in a rainforest that provides everything the tree needs in order to grow, bloom, and produce the seed pods that people harvest to make chocolate.

[Point out the appropriate latitudes around the equator on the world map depicting chocolate-producing regions.]

Everything in the ecosystem works together for good, just as our Creator God planned. If we think about it, the Church is like a rainforest. The water of baptism and the warmth of the Holy Spirit unite God's people. Each of us plays a different but important role in the ecosystem called the Church. The Church doesn't only exist near the equator though. God's Church is scattered all over the world. However, in order to survive the temptations of the world, the Church must remain close to God. God is like the equator—the source that runs through the middle of everything we are and everything we do. So now you know the first Lenten lesson: Where does chocolate grow? The rainforest! Where do Christians grow? The Church!

Pray

Dear God, Thank You for creating all the right conditions for us to grow in faith. Help us to value the role each one plays in your Church. Amen.

Taste

Milk chocolate bars

Do This Week

Design a triptych on paper folded into thirds. In each section, draw a representation of the story of Jesus' temptation, recorded in Mark 1:12-13.

Discover what kinds of opportunities exist in denominational missions within the rainforest regions of the world.

Look on a world map to identify all the countries that exist within the chocolate-growing regions of the earth.

Make triple-chocolate "temptation" brownies with chocolate syrup, chocolate chips, and chocolate frosting. Discuss the meaning of the word temptation and the importance of learning from Jesus what is best to resist.

Read about life in the rainforest for plants, animals, and people.

Write a modern day interpretation of the Biblical story about temptation. Translate the devil's suggestions for Jesus into situations we might be tempted by today.

Family Devotions
Second Sunday in Lent: Know How

Read

Mark 8:31-38
Romans 4:13-25

Say

Know How
Know How being different is a blessing
Our Lenten commitment to "know chocolate" challenges us to embrace the differences that make God's creation unique – both for the cacao tree and for the Christian disciple.

Show

Cacao tree with blossoms and pods

Say

The know chocolate question for this Second Sunday in Lent is how does chocolate grow? Can you imagine what a chocolate plant might look like?

[Hold up a picture or model of a cacao tree with blossoms and pods.]

Did your imagined tree look like this? The cacao tree blossoms all year long, and the blossoms occur any place on the tree. Flying all around are the tiny midge flies that pollinate the blossoms that bloom everywhere and all the time! The more we know the story of chocolate, the more connections we have to think about during Lent. Like the cacao tree, we should blossom with the beauty of God's presence in our lives all the time. We should stay attached directly to God, just like the flowers on the trunk of the cacao tree. And the problems that beset us in life are like the midge flies—they help us produce the fruit of faith. Jesus challenges us to pick up our cross in life and follow in faith. If we do that, then our lives, too, will produce fruit that benefits the world around us. So where do Christians bloom? Everywhere! And when? All the time!

Pray

Dear God, Thank You for Your love that flows through us all the time. Help us to blossom with faith everywhere we go. Amen.

Taste

M&M'S®

Do This Week

Interview people in the congregation or the family to discover how faith makes a difference in life. Write brief faith biographies to display with each person's picture. Create a bulletin board designed as a "rainforest" of ever-blossoming believers.

Listen to a collection of sounds from the rainforest. Use creative movement to show a cacao plant growing into a fruitful tree.

Look in a hymnal for songs about growing in the Christian faith. Sing a favorite or learn a new song together.

Make a football-shaped puppet to tell the story of the cacao plant and its message for the Christian life.

Melt chocolate, pour into cross-shaped molds, and let harden. Give a chocolate cross and share the Bible story with someone.

View photographs of the stages in the growth of the cacao pod.

Family Devotions
Third Sunday in Lent: Know Which

Read

John 2:13-22
1 Corinthians 1:18-25

Say

Know Which
Know Which part of life is most important
Our Lenten commitment to "know chocolate" challenges us to envision the potential for changing the world — both with chocolate and with God's love.

Show

Open cacao pod revealing seeds

Say

Which do the pods from the cacao plant produce—beans or seeds?

[Hold up a picture or a model of an open cacao pod revealing seeds.]

Although some people might call what is inside each pod a bean, we will call them seeds because they can be planted to produce more cacao trees. Each football-shaped cacao pod contains about thirty to fifty almond-sized seeds. About 2,000 years ago, the ancient people known as the Maya began planting seeds from the cacao tree in their gardens. The Mayans influenced the Aztecs who taught the Spanish who shared both the seeds and the recipe for drinking chocolate with all of Europe. Whether you call them beans or seeds, what is inside the cacao pod is the most important part because from them we make chocolate and grow more cacao trees! Just think—one pod produces thirty to fifty seeds, but one seed can produce a tree that produces hundreds of pods that each contain thirty to fifty seeds! The first Mayan gardeners could not have imagined how planting one seed could change the world! All because someone realized that what is on the inside matters most.

During Lent, we realize that each of us is like a seed. When we have Jesus' love on the inside, we have the power and wisdom of God within us! That means we can produce lots of fruit! Fruit that will not only bless us, but also many others in ways that we cannot even imagine. So we learn that—for the cacao pod and for the Christian—what's on the inside matters most!

Pray

Dear God, Thank You for Jesus' love that fills us with Your goodness. Help us to share what Jesus gives us with the world. Amen.

Taste

Chocolate covered cacao or coffee beans

Do This Week

Find a recipe for chocolate cupcakes with cream filling. Make a batch to share.

Gather a variety of seeds to create seed-art pictures. Invite artists to create a design that represents the message "What's on the inside matters most!"

Make music with gourds, rain-sticks, or other seed-filled containers.

Play a game of "Inside Out" by placing ten items in a cloth or paper bag. Challenge the participants to pull out one item at a time and name a way to use it to change the world.

Read the book *Harvest of Hope* by Phil Grout (Madison, WI: SERRV International, 2003) to learn about the process of harvesting cacao pods and their seeds.

Write a shape poem in the almond-shaped pattern of the cacao seed. Use the shape to express the importance of an inner life filled with love from God.

Family Devotions
Fourth Sunday in Lent: Know When

Read

John 3:14-21
Ephesians 2:1-10

Say

Know When
Know When it's time to share good news
Our Lenten commitment to "know chocolate" challenges us to share goodness with the world – both the recipes for chocolate delicacies and God's good news of Jesus Christ.

Show

Cacao beans ready for fermenting

Say

The known story of chocolate starts about the same time Jesus was born with the ancient Mayan people who first enjoyed drinking chocolate. Mayan priests used a chocolate drink during special religious ceremonies. Later, the Aztecs conquered the Mayans, and then the Spanish conquered the Aztec Empire. The Spanish first brought the recipe for the Aztec chocolate drink to Europe. But only the wealthy people across Europe could afford to enjoy it. When is it okay to keep something God-given a secret or to use God's gifts just for ourselves? Never! Chocolate is always for sharing.

When a Dutch scientist named Coenraad Van Houten invented a machine called the chocolate press, this new invention allowed people to press the cocoa beans to make bars of chocolate and cocoa powder. Then chocolate could be stored easily and produced more cheaply. At last, chocolate was available to everyone. Is the message of Easter just for a chosen few? No! The Bible gives us God's recipe for hope—and it's no secret! John 3:16 tells us that God loves the world. Jesus died for everyone's sins and God raised Jesus up so that the whole world could know God's power over sin and death. So if chocolate is always for sharing, what about God's love? God's love is always for sharing, too! Now you can share God's recipe for hope with the world!

Pray

Dear God, Thank You for sending Jesus for the whole world. Help us to share Your recipe for hope with everyone who hungers for it. Amen.

Taste

Hot chocolate mix

Do This Week

Design a recipe card to share God's message found in John 3:16. Make up ideas for each element of a recipe—such as ingredients and methods to process them. Be sure to include "Serves: the world."

Enjoy music from the countries that produce chocolate, such as *Music from the Chocolate Lands*.

Find a recipe for making powered chocolate drink mix. Make a batch and package it as gifts.

Research all the ways cocoa butter is used in lotions, foods, and other modern products.

Visit a paint-your-own ceramics shop and design a mug or pot for enjoying hot chocolate.

Write an imaginative story of the Spanish princess who chose to give away her family's secret recipe as a treasure for her new husband's family.

Family Devotions
Fifth Sunday in Lent: Know Why

Read

Luke 17:6-7
Hebrews 11:1-3

Say

Know Why
Know Why health benefits both body and soul
Our Lenten commitment to "know chocolate" challenges us to understand that God wants us to be healthy – both physically and spiritually.

Show

Dried cacao beans

Say

The more scientists do research about chocolate, the more they discover the benefits chocolate can bring.

[Point to a picture of dried cacao beans.]

In order to make chocolate, the seeds of the cacao plant must be dried in the sun so that they become rich brown beans with a hard outer shell. It is the inside of the cacao bean that holds the health benefits found in chocolate. The flavonoids in cacao beans improve blood flow to the brain, help provide a sense of well being, and contribute to better heart health. Wow! Now we know why we like chocolate so much! Chocolate can be good for us!

However, the darker the chocolate we eat, the better it is for us. Dark chocolate contains more of the cacao bean and less sugar, milk fat, or other additives. Some experts suggest that one ounce of dark chocolate per day is a good way to stay healthy.

Faith has also proven to be good for us. Studies indicate that people who make faith, prayer, and Church attendance a priority have the same health advantages as people who exercise regularly and who don't smoke. Just as more cacao in chocolate is healthy for us, the more God is a part of our lives the more healthy we will be. Not only is chocolate good for us, faith is good for us!

Pray

Dear God, Thank You for the ways You provide to keep us healthy in body and in spirit. Amen.

Taste

Dark chocolate bar

Do This Week

Discover the drying power of the sun by creating a sun picture on photosensitive paper or on black or dark blue construction paper. Lay natural items such as leaves, twigs, or seeds in a pleasing arrangement on the paper and place the creation in a sunny location for a period of time. Remove the items and see the shapes created as the sun faded the background paper.

Enjoy a chocolate tasting party. Sample chocolate with differing levels of cacao content and determine a favorite.

Learn more about the health benefits of chocolate from an article on a website or a discussion with a family doctor or health teacher.

Make a chart of all the activities at Church that are healthy for our faith. Select activities such as sing in the choir and list benefits like sing the Scripture, praise God, learn words to prayers.

Read about the processing of chocolate, especially about the fermenting and drying process of the cacao bean.

Visit a nursery to see if they sell cocoa bean shells to spread in a garden.

Family Devotions
Sixth Sunday in Lent (Palm Sunday/Passion Sunday): Know So

Read

Matthew 21:1-11
Philippians 2:5-11

Say

Know So
Know So choices can be based on wisdom
Our commitment to "know chocolate" challenges us to distinguish the genuine from the imitation — both in types of chocolates and in those we choose to follow.

Show

Crushed cacao beans

Say

The process of making chocolate has only just begun when the dried beans are sent to be roasted and crushed. First the beans must be winnowed to remove the hard outer shell. The inner part called the nib is then crushed to extract the cocoa butter or oil from the bean. Then the cocoa butter and the crushed nibs are mixed together again to make chocolate.

[Display the picture of crushed cacao beans.]

Low quality chocolate is processed more quickly and can have many other ingredients added to it. That is why we must read the ingredient list and carefully choose genuine chocolate.

On this Palm Sunday we celebrate the story of Jesus coming into Jerusalem as God's chosen, the Messiah. The people in the crowd on Palm Sunday didn't choose wisely. They thought Jesus was coming into Jerusalem to be their earthly king. The people hadn't read God's description carefully enough. God sent Jesus to rule in our hearts, not on a throne. On Palm Sunday we begin Holy Week—a time to remember why Jesus came and why He had to suffer death on a cross. Jesus accepted what happened to Him in the time we call Holy Week because He loves us. We must choose wisely and accept Jesus as our Savior.

Pray

Dear God, Thank You for the power to choose. Help us to recognize the very best gift of all—Your Son, Jesus. Amen.

Taste

Mini-chocolate bars

Do This Week

Compare ingredients listed on a variety of candy bar wrappers to find those with the best chocolate content. Remember that the ingredients are listed in descending amounts.

Create placemats to use on Easter Sunday that depict the events of Holy Week from Palm Sunday to Easter morning.

Design a mosaic cross by gluing crushed cacao beans or cocoa shells in a cross-shaped pattern on paper or a tile.

Sing a song about choices such as "I Have Decided to Follow Jesus."

View the Palm Sunday scene from a film on the life of Christ.

Write a "Choose Your Own Adventure" story about people in the crowd during the first Palm Sunday. Stop the account at a critical point and create two options for the character's actions. Write both outcomes for readers to select. What would be the difference between choosing to believe Jesus or choosing to shout "Crucify him!"?

Family Devotions
Maundy Thursday: Know By

Read

John 13:21-30
1 Corinthians 11:23-26

Say

Know By
Know By remembering Jesus' words and deeds
Our Lenten commitment to "know chocolate" challenges us to remember those we love on special occasions – both with gifts of chocolate and with gifts of bread and cup.

Show

Advertisement for heart-shaped box of chocolates

Say

We can know quality chocolate by reading the ingredients, but we also know what chocolate is best by the advertising. Until the 1850s, chocolate was available only as a drink. Then some English folks named Cadbury discovered how to make a bar of chocolate. Later, some people in Switzerland named Nestle added milk to create milk chocolate. So not much more than a hundred years ago, the first advertisements were created for boxes of chocolate to give as gifts to loved ones. Often, the boxes in advertisements were shaped like a heart.

[Hold up a heart-shaped box of chocolates.]

That symbol suggests that chocolate is a gift worth remembering!

During Holy Week, Maundy Thursday is about a gift worth remembering, as well. We celebrate the day when Jesus ate the Passover Meal with His disciples before He was arrested and crucified. Jesus told His followers that they should remember two symbols: the bread that He broke with them and the cup that He shared with them. Today we still use the symbolic meal of bread and cup as a way to remember Christ's gift of sacrifice for us. Just like a heart-shaped box represents a loving remembrance, so do the symbols of bread and cup. If chocolate is a gift worth remembering, what can we say about the message of Maundy Thursday? Jesus is a gift worth remembering!

Pray

Dear God, We are grateful that You love us. We promise to remember what Jesus did to show us Your love. Amen.

Taste

Chocolate from a heart-shaped box of candy

Do This Week

Attend a Maundy Thursday service and listen for the words Jesus spoke to His disciples about remembering Him through the elements of bread and cup.

Design a poster as an advertisement for God's message of love found in Jesus' life, death, and resurrection. What symbols would best communicate that message?

Look in a hymnal for songs about communion. Select one to learn to sing as a family remembrance.

Make heart-shaped molded chocolates as a gift for people who need to hear that they are loved.

Recreate a Passover Meal following the traditional Jewish Seder.

Search for advertisements for chocolate in books, magazines, or on the Internet. Look for early advertisements from the 1800s; try to find advertising examples from around the world; or discover as many different modern advertisements as possible.

Family Devotions
Good Friday: Know That

Read

John 19:16-18
Hebrews 10:19-23

Say

Know That
Know That something bitter can make things better
Our Lenten commitment to "know chocolate" challenges us to accept that God can use what is bitter to produce something good—both in the taste of chocolate and in the life of Jesus.

Show

Symbol for fair trade chocolate

Say

If chocolate is so good, why did the Aztecs call it *xocóatl* [sho-CO-lah-tul]—"bitter water"? Have you ever tasted baking chocolate or other chocolate that contains little or no sugar? Chocolate's unique flavor combines well with sweeteners to make a rich tasting treat—but without added ingredients it would taste very bitter. Without that bitter under-taste, however, chocolate would not be as pleasing to our palates. In cooking, as well as in life, something bitter can make things better.

We might be tempted to think, "How can the day that Jesus died be called Good?" That was a bitter experience. The more we read and learn about the story of Good Friday, the more we understand what Jesus had to suffer. If Jesus did not experience death, then we would not know the joy of His resurrection on Easter morning and we would not have the assurance of how much God loves us and is willing to forgive us. That makes the day of Jesus' death a Good Friday for us—we are saved, forgiven, and assured that we, too, will be raised to new life in eternity.

Chocolate, too, has gone through some tragic times. Because of people's love for chocolate and because it grew only near the equator, many countries made colonies of the chocolate-growing regions. That meant people growing the chocolate often worked and slaved so that other people could enjoy chocolate delights. Today many chocolate farmers still make so little they can not afford to buy the chocolate they produce. But God can also use us to turn something bitter into something better. We can buy fair trade chocolate and work to make sure big companies are paying fair prices for the chocolate they buy. Because Jesus made sacrifices for us, we can find the courage to make sacrifices to help make the world a better place for everyone. With God's help, we, too, can turn something bitter into something better.

Taste

Fair trade chocolate

Pray

Dear God, Thank You for sending Jesus to give us hope that the bitter things of life can be made better. This Good Friday send us the strength to continue Your work in changing the world for the better. Amen.

Do This Week

Locate a book of art reproductions that feature artist's interpretations of the crucifixion. Compare the details in the artwork to the words found in the Biblical account.

Look for recipes that require unsweetened baking chocolate. Taste the mixture before and after sweeteners are added.

Make a life map of personal experiences—a sequence of events and choices over a period of time. Place an X at points that represent a bitter experience. Write a story that explains this life experience, but focuses on the ways the bitter time was transformed into something good—a lesson learned, a blessing discovered, or an unexpected opportunity that occurred as a result.

Read the story of the crucifixion and the events surrounding Jesus' last Friday by dividing the nineteenth chapter of John into four sections: John 19:1-16, 17-27, 28-37, and 38-42. Pause after each segment to discuss what happened, to ask questions, to discuss what the people in the story were thinking and feeling, and to consider how the actions of Jesus impact our lives today.

Research the current chocolate production process to discover how fair-trade prices are making a difference for the lives of chocolate farmers.

Visit an import store with fair-trade goods such as 10,000 Villages to purchase samples of chocolate products.

Family Devotions
Easter Sunday: Know Who

Read

John 20:1-18
1 Corinthians 15:1-11

Say

Know Who
Know Who calls us to follow in faith
Our Lenten commitment to "know chocolate" challenges us to learn the difference that can happen when we are open to change—just like the process that can make white chocolate or the miracle of resurrection that can make new life.

Show

Final product

Say

Hallelujah! Christ is risen! He is risen, indeed! This is the traditional Easter greeting among Christians around the world. The bitter news of Good Friday has turned into the sweet rejoicing of Easter morning. We have shared what it means to know chocolate for six long weeks of Lent, preparing for this special day. We have seen chocolate through all the stages of its growth, its harvesting, its processing, and its advertising. Now we can see the final product.

[Display white chocolate bunny, cross, egg, or lamb.]

But when in the process does chocolate turn white?

Manufacturers can add as much of the crushed nibs back into the cocoa butter as they choose. That is how they make different levels of cacao flavor—from light to dark chocolate. But there is one more option—not adding any of the nibs at all. If manufacturers add sugar and flavorings only to the separated cocoa butter, the result is what people call white chocolate. And white chocolate certainly looks different!

Jesus looked different to the disciples after His resurrection, as well. In the story of the first Easter morning, Mary Magdalene thought Jesus was the gardener when she first encountered Him near the empty tomb. Jesus had been buried as a human being, but He was raised by God's power as our Messiah, our Savior. That must have been quite a transformation process—sort of like the crushing process that separates the dark outer part of the cocoa bean from the inner essence of cocoa butter. White chocolate can remind us that we have an inner essence, a spirit, as well. The Easter story shows us that God offers us the gift of eternal life. The same resurrection power that raised Jesus from the dead will separate the outer shell of our physical bodies from our inner spirit—the part of us that God keeps alive. Just like in the Easter story, when Jesus calls Mary's name and she recognizes Him, Jesus calls our names, too. And when we understand Easter's message, we say: Hallelujah! Christ is risen! He is risen, indeed!

Taste

White chocolate bunny, cross, egg, or lamb

Pray

Dear God, Thank You for raising Jesus to new life. We say yes to Christ's call to believe and follow Him. Amen.

Do This Week

Develop a list of questions to ask and then talk with someone who has traveled to Israel and visited the places where Jesus walked and taught. If there are no persons available who have visited Jerusalem, look for a travelogue about Israel in the local library.

Make molded white chocolates to give as Easter gifts to family, friends, and neighbors.

Read all the Gospel accounts of the resurrection. Discuss the similarities and differences. Ask the participants which ones make them feel most connected to the Easter message and why.

Research photos and/or paintings of the "Garden Tomb." Learn about the traditions that have developed around historic sites in Israel believed to be the location of Christ's resurrection.

Sing a favorite Easter hymn such as "He Lives" or "Up from the Grave He Arose." Discuss how the music matches the emotions we experience in response to the Easter message.

View Easter scenes from a film or films about the life of Christ. Focus especially on the scene between Mary and Jesus when she recognizes who He is. Discuss moments when viewers have sensed the presence of the risen Christ.

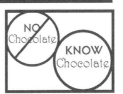

Banner or Posters

Illustrations/Patterns

Ash Wednesday: Know What

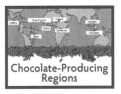

First Sunday in Lent: Know Where

Second Sunday in Lent: Know How

Third Sunday in Lent: Know Which

Fourth Sunday in Lent: Know When

Fifth Sunday in Lent: Know Why

Sixth Sunday in Lent (Palm Sunday/Passion Sunday): Know So

Maundy Thursday: Know By

Good Friday: Know That

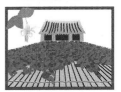

Easter Sunday: Know Who

Banner or Posters

Banner

A banner provides an effective way to enhance a seasonal theme. It can be constructed from a variety of materials. Fabric will add warmth to architectural space and last for many years; paper allows for quick, inexpensive designs.

Consider where the banner will hang to determine the size, shape, and color. Be sure that banner lettering and symbols are large enough to be seen from a distance and that colors do not clash with surrounding decor.

This seasonal banner follows the theme developed in *Know Chocolate for Lent*, with a symbol or phrase added each Sunday and special day of Lent and Easter.

Materials needed include:

- Copy machine;
- Dressmaker's chalk;
- Fabric, felt, or paper for symbols and words;
- Fabric or paper for banner background -- at least 3 feet by 5 feet;
- Glue or bonding material;
- Illustrations/patterns for symbols from *Know Chocolate* series (Pages 90-99);
- Iron;
- Paint (Optional);
- Paper;
- Pencils;
- Pins or Velcro® dots (Optional);
- Rod or cord for hanging banner;
- Scissors;
- Sewing machine;
- Symbol patterns;
- Thread.

Before the first worship service, prepare the background material for the banner by hemming the edges and forming a casing for the rod. Hems and rod pockets can be stitched, glued, or ironed in place with fusible web. Follow instructions on fusible product for bonding two pieces of fabric.

Prepare ten blocks, one to convey the symbol for each of the six weeks of Lent plus the special days of Ash Wednesday, Maundy Thursday, Good Friday, and Easter Sunday, to attach to the banner background. Photocopy or phototransfer one illustration/pattern from the Enhancements section of this resource on each of the blocks. Decide how to affix each illustrated block to the banner by sewing, gluing, or bonding them to the material. Place the first block, for Ash Wednesday, with the words Know Chocolate in the top center of the banner. Each week add the appropriate block, grouping them in rows of threes.

Display the banner on a specially constructed banner stand or hang it where it will enhance the worship environment. Be sure that symbols can be added easily throughout the seasons.

Posters

Follow the directions for creating a banner, only duplicate the illustrations provided for the Sundays and special days of Lent and Easter and attach each to a separate piece of poster board to display during the children's message or in a worship center arrangement.

Illustrations/Patterns
Ash Wednesday
Know What

NO Chocolate/KNOW Chocolate

Illustrations/Patterns
First Sunday in Lent
Know Where

World map depicting chocolate-producing regions

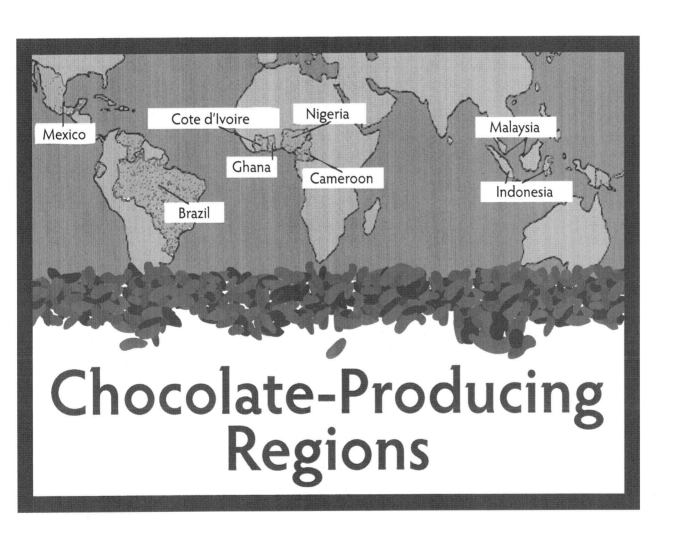

Illustrations/Patterns
Second Sunday in Lent
Know How

Cacao tree with blossoms and pods

Illustrations/Patterns
Third Sunday in Lent
Know Which

Open cacao pod revealing seeds

Enhancements

Illustrations/Patterns
Fourth Sunday in Lent
Know When

Cacao beans ready for fermenting

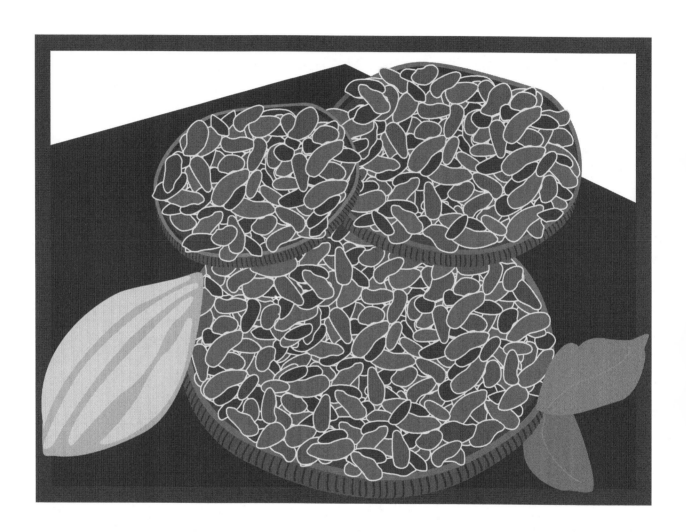

Illustrations/Patterns
Fifth Sunday in Lent
Know Why

Dried cacao beans

Illustrations/Patterns
Sixth Sunday in Lent (Palm Sunday/Passion Sunday)
Know So

Crushed cacao beans

Illustrations/Patterns
Maundy Thursday
Know By

Advertisement for heart-shaped box of chocolates

Illustrations/Patterns
Good Friday
Know That

Symbol for fair trade chocolate

Illustrations/Patterns
Easter Sunday
Know Who

Final product – chocolate bunny, cross, egg, or lamb

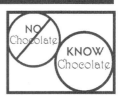

Chocolate's Religious Roots

Historical Timeline for Chocolate

Scripture

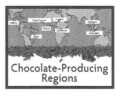

Chocolate's Religious Roots

The ancient Maya priests of Central America presented a chocolate drink at sacred altars during special religious ceremonies. They also made offerings of cacao seeds to the gods.

The Aztecs—who learned to enjoy chocolate from the Maya—presented offerings of cacao to their god Quetzalcoatl (ket sal koh AH tul), who is often depicted as a feathered serpent. According to one Aztec legend, the god Quetzalcoatl brought heavenly cacao to earth. Eventually, Quetzalcoatl was cast out of paradise for the blasphemous act of giving this sacred drink to humans because the gods felt that only they should have access to chocolate.

Both Aztec and Mayan religious rituals and banquets included chocolate as a part of their celebrations. It was mixed into a liquid used to 'baptize' young boys and girls and to toast at weddings.

Hernán Cortés brought cacao seeds back to Spain when his army conquered the Aztec civilization. The Spanish monks added sugar and cinnamon as they experimented with the recipe for the chocolate drink. The monks kept the recipe Spain's secret for one hundred years.

The Latin name for the cacao plant is *Theobroma Cacao*: literally "the food of the gods."

No fewer than seven popes made pronouncements on chocolate, all agreeing that it does not break the Lenten fast.

In the 1650s the Society of Jesus issued an act prohibiting Jesuits from drinking chocolate. Embarrassingly, they had to rescind the edict as many students started leaving in protest.

Quaker families Frys of Bristol, Cadburys of Birmingham, and Rowntrees of York pioneered modern chocolate production in the 1800s.

Historical Timeline for Chocolate

250 – 900

Maya civilization reaches its height, people begin gathering cacao seeds from rainforest trees and planting this important crop in household gardens; the word chocolate comes from the Maya word *xocoatl* which means bitter water; carvings of cacao pods are represented in stone carvings of Mayan temples, symbolizing life and fertility; literary texts refer to *xocoatl* as "the gods' food."

1200

Aztec people trade for cacao seeds with their Maya neighbors to the south, eventually subjugating the Maya culture and demanding payment in cacao; cacao beans become the form of currency for the Aztec vast trade empire.

1492

Columbus returns from America bringing a few dark brown cacao beans among his treasures, but no one takes much notice.

1528

Cortez presents the Spanish King, Charles V, with cocoa beans from the New World and the necessary tools for its preparation as a spicy drink; the Spaniards mix the ground beans with sugar, vanilla, nutmeg, cloves, allspice, and cinnamon and keep their chocolate recipe a secret from the rest of the world for almost one-hundred years; its use was considered medicinal and its oversight given to monks.

1569

Pope Pius V declares that drinking chocolate on Friday did not break the Lenten Fast.

1643

The Spanish Princess Maria Theresa is betrothed to Louis XIV of France and gives her fiancé an engagement gift of chocolate, packaged in an elegantly ornate chest.

1657

London's first chocolate shop is opened by a Frenchman. London Chocolate Houses become the trendy meeting places for the elite London society to savor their new luxury. The first chocolate house opens in London advertising "this excellent West India drink."

1662

Rome reiterates that a chocolate drink does not break the Lenten fast.

1732

Steam-driven chocolate mill invented; grinds up cacao seeds faster and makes it possible to produce large amounts of chocolate inexpensively.

1765

First chocolate factory in the U.S.A. at Dorchester, Massachusetts.

1828

Dutch scientist Coenraad Van Houten invents the chocolate press. Still used today, this machine squeezes out cocoa butter and makes it possible to produce solid chocolate as well as cocoa powder.

1847

The Fry and Sons Company of Bristol, England, introduces the first chocolate bar meant for eating as a snack.

1849

Domingo Ghirardelli moves from Latin America to San Francisco to sell supplies to miners with gold rush fever. But having seen cacao growing in Guatemala, he soon started a chocolate factory instead.

1868

Richard Cadbury, the founder of England's Cadbury chocolate company, introduces the first Valentine's Day candy box.

1875

Daniel Peter from Switzerland puts the first milk chocolate on the market.

1890

Robert Stroehecker is the "father" of the first chocolate Easter bunny.

1894

The Hershey Chocolate Company is founded in Pennsylvania by Milton Hershey.

1913

Jules Sechaud of Montreux of Switzerland introduces the process for filling chocolates.

1918 and 1942

During both world wars, the United States Armed Forces includes chocolate in the rations of U.S. soldiers; Army D-rations still include three four-ounce bars of chocolate; chocolate is also taken into space as part of the diet of U.S. astronauts.

Sources

The Chicago Field Museum. All about Chocolate. "History of Chocolate."

http://www.fieldmuseum.org/Chocolate/history.html

CocoaJava.com. "Chocolate's History: A Timeline of Invention and Discovery."

http://cocoajava.com/cocoa_timeline.html

The Gourmet Chocolate of the Month Club. "Chocolate History."

http://www.chocolatemonthclub.com/chocolatehistory.htm

Scripture

Matthew 6:1-6, 16-21

Ash Wednesday: Know What

Matthew 21:1-11

Sixth Sunday in Lent (Palm Sunday/Passion Sunday): Know So

Mark 1:9-15

First Sunday in Lent: Know Where

Mark 8:31-38

Second Sunday in Lent: Know How

Luke 17:6-7

Fifth Sunday in Lent: Know Why

John 2:13-22

Third Sunday in Lent: Know Which

John 3:14-21

Fourth Sunday in Lent: Know When

John 13:21-30

Maundy Thursday: Know By

John 19:16-18

   Good Friday: Know That

John 20:1-18

   Easter Sunday: Know Who

Romans 4:13-25

   Second Sunday in Lent: Know How

1 Corinthians 1:18-25

   Third Sunday in Lent: Know Which

1 Corinthians 11:23-26

   Maundy Thursday: Know By

1 Corinthians 15:1-11

   Easter Sunday: Know Who

2 Corinthians 5:20b-6:10

   Ash Wednesday: Know What

Ephesians 2:1-10

   Fourth Sunday in Lent: Know When

Philippians 2:5-11

   Sixth Sunday in Lent (Palm Sunday/Passion Sunday): Know So

Hebrews 10:19-23

   Good Friday: Know That

Hebrews 11:1-3

   Fifth Sunday in Lent: Know Why

1 Peter 3:18-22

   First Sunday in Lent: Know Where

Anna L. Liechty

Ann Liechty is a National Board Certified teacher and retired chair of the English Department at Plymouth High School in Indiana. She has also worked as a Religious Education volunteer, teaching all levels, directing Sunday morning and youth programming, consulting with congregations about their educational ministry, and writing a wide variety of religious education materials. She serves as Vice President of Active Learning Associates, Inc. Ann lives in Plymouth, Indiana, with her husband Ron, a retired pastor. They have five children, ten grandchildren, and three great-grandchildren.

Phyllis Vos Wezeman

Phyllis Wezeman is President of Active Learning Associates, Inc. and Director of Christian Nurture at First Presbyterian Church in South Bend, Indiana. Phyllis has served as Adjunct Faculty in the Education Department at Indiana University and the Department of Theology at the University of Notre Dame. She has taught at the Saint Petersburg (Russia) State University, the Shanghai (China) Teacher's University, and for the Church of Central Africa Presbyterian (C.C.A.P.) in Malawi, Africa. Phyllis, who holds an M.S. in Education from Indiana University, is a recipient of three "Distinguished Alumna Awards" from her high school and university. Author or co-author of numerous books and articles, Phyllis and her husband, Ken, have three children and five grandchildren.

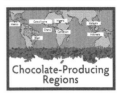

Chocolate-Producing Regions

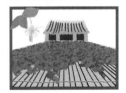

Made in the USA
Lexington, KY
07 January 2011